BIG BANG

CANNONS

THE CARBIDE CANNON,
A UNIQUE
AMERICAN TOY

BY

RAYMOND V. BRANDES

RAY VIN

RAY-VIN PUBLISHING CO., NEW BRUNSWICK, NEW JERSEY

CHAPTER ONE
A LOVE AFFAIR

My name is Raymond Brandes and my love for toy cannons goes back to my childhood. It all began Christmas 1957 when Mom and Dad gave me a BIG-BANG Motor Tank. It had a hull of cast iron with solid rubber wheels.

The Home Town Ordnance Squad. Fred(l) and Ray(r) Posing in 1957.

What a great toy for a boy of nine. My brother Fred had a 10FC from his previous birthday, July 5th. In spite of the cold, we took our BIG-BANGS outside where we fired them until we were numb. Later, we posed with our cannons for a photo in the back yard.

Being an impulsive kid, I didn't do much unless there was immediate gratification. Bangsite was not available in stores and had to be mail ordered. I distrusted the mail and mail ordering. In spite of all this, Bangsite was mail ordered once. When that supply was exhausted, the tank was neglected. The loose parts disappeared and then one day the tank was gone.

Cannons knew that I liked them and they seemed to find me. Cannons arrived as gifts, cannons were acquired at flea markets and yard sales. I even made a few powder cannons during my years as a machinist.

My collector status became official in October 1988 when I bought a complete BIG-BANG 60MM for $8.00 at a flea market. This was a good buy as these are generally priced about $20.00 to $30.00 and usually missing parts.

My wife Vincentine was extremely amused by my explanation of how it worked and that for ammunition it used "Bangsite". I was being too serious and we went back and forth for a while and it ended with me saying she did not know what Bangsite was or even where to get it. Little did I know...

Christmas morning 1988. Vince surprised me with a brand new BIG-BANG 10FC and extra Bangsite.

Vince already had these gifts wrapped the day we got the 60MM and that was why she laughed out loud when I so smugly implied she was clueless! Later that day, our friend Ed Boganski came over and we fired the 60MM and the 10FC in the basement. The concussion caused a snow flurry of loose white paint from the joists!

My collection grew over the next two years. However, only two of some sixty cannons were carbide cannons. The entire collection was proudly displayed in a three shelf barrister bookcase.

April 1990 saw us on the road to Renninger's Antique Market in Adamstown, Pennsylvania with our friends Ed and Joan Glaser. Ed and Joan insisted on stopping at Shupp's Grove and we did. Having been to Renninger's before and wanting to be there again made me impatient and annoyed about this Shupp's Grove place. I didn't know it then, but this change in plans was going to change my life.

We did not know what it was, but Vince found it way down the back side of a vendor's table where it could not be seen from the main aisle.

It was big, it was cast iron and it was so nose heavy that it would only sit with the muzzle on the ground. The paint was old and finely checked from age. The large red wheels had eight spokes and looked vaguely familiar.

It was definitely a carbide gun having a breach opening with locking lugs and a water reservoir. No breach block was present. Why was it so nose heavy? Could an elaborate (and heavy) breach block be the missing component in this balancing act? It would be quite a while before this mystery was resolved. We didn't know at the time, but the axles were broken and the wheels were mounted improperly rearward causing the imbalance.

The Distraught, yet Majestic, 16F.

After careful consideration we bought the cannon if for no other reason than that it was a carbide cannon like none we had ever seen before.

When we got it home, the familiar note about the wheels became apparent. The wheels had the same tear drop cut-outs as the wheels on our BIG-BANG 10FC, only these wheels were much larger.

The reply to my letter to BIG-BANG confirmed that it was a model 16F and the good people at Conestoga, makers of the BIG-BANG, were re-manufacturing breach blocks for these old guns. Also enclosed was a photo copy of an ad from *TOY WORLD*, Sept. 1929 showing all manner of BIG-BANGS. Illustrated were several cannon, a pistol, a gun boat, even an airplane!!!

I was hooked. How many of these other old pieces were out there waiting all these years for me to find them and give them a warm home? What other carbide guns existed that I did not know about? Was Conestoga the only manufacture of carbide cannons? I had to know....

The Classic BIG-BANG Tear Drop Wheel.

September, 1929 Toy World 87

Birthdays---

FIELD ARTILLERY
No. 16F—23 in. $5.50
No. 12F—17 in. 3.75
No. 8F—11 in. 2.25
No. 6F—9 in. 1.50
Mounted on two large red artillery wheels.

HEAVY ARTILLERY
No. 10W—14 in. .... $[illegible].00
Mounted on steel carriage. Four red artillery wheels.

BOMBING PLANE
No. 11P—Length 11 in., Wing Spread 13 in. $3.50
Modeled after latest stream line design. Each "Bang" rotates propeller.

NAVY GUN-BOAT
No. 9B—9 in. .... [illegible]
Mounted on four wheels.

SAFETY PISTOL
No. 6P—8 in. $2.00
Comes in leather holster. Looks and sounds like a real pistol but is safe.

BANGSITE—the Safe Ammunition—per tube .... $ .15

SPARK PLUGS—per card .... $ .10

BIG-BANG

A BIRTHDAY is such a *big* event in a child's life . . . . ranking with those other great days of Christmas and Fourth of July. Why shouldn't the sturdy son who's *"just six years old today"* (and, oh, so proud of it!) be permitted to celebrate in a manner befitting the occasion?

He should . . . . for all too soon birthdays lose their zest.

BIG-BANG Safe Celebrators are particularly apropos as birthday gifts for young boys, because they provide a *safe* means of signalizing an occurrence of so great importance.

NO MATCHES - NO POWDER

SAFE NOISE

THE CONESTOGA CORPORATION
Main Office and Factory:
Bethlehem, Pa., U. S. A.

EXPORT DEPARTMENT:
Office No. 605, 130 Pearl Street, New York City

Toy World Ad, September 1929.

Note the wheel location on the 16F (bottom left). To keep the muzzle off the ground the ammo chest was filled with lead shot.

CHAPTER TWO

JAMES H. WILY & THE BIG-BANG

James Hunter Wily, one of five sons of George and Adeline Wily, was born on a Chester County farm near Pughtown, Pennsylvania on July 12, 1879.

Young Wily, About 1911.

James attended West Chester Normal School (now West Chester State Teachers College) and in 1903 matriculated at Lehigh University in Bethlehem where he founded and was a charter member of Sigma Phi Epsilon. Hunter, as his family called him, graduated with the degree Electrical Engineer in 1905.

Young Wily immediately joined the Lehigh teaching staff and in 1909 was appointed assistant professor in the physics department where he served until 1920 when he resigned to devote full time to his business.

From newspaper accounts we know Professor Wily had his own lab and office. On his desk he kept a brass carbide cannon of his own design. Naturally visitors would inquire about the cannon which Wily would then demonstrate.

Dr. Emery

Dr. Natt Emery, then vice president of Lehigh, visited Professor Wily's office and like other visitors was curious about the cannon. Like the others he jumped when the cannon was fired. Dr. Emery asked Professor Wily why he did not market the toy.

Wily was having fun with his cannon and gave no thought to the commercial possibilities. The following Fourth of July Dr. Emery visited Wily again.

Professor Wily, 1913.

This time Dr. Emery used a different approach. He told Wily that it was his duty to put the toy on the market, thereby making available a substitute to the dangerous fireworks that maimed and killed boys every year.

Wily had his own experience with being maimed. When he was only five he took advantage of a post holiday sale and bought three packs of caps for a penny on July 5th and put them in his pocket. In those days, caps were charged with much more powder than they are now and probably a less stable compound as well. Somehow the caps exploded and left Wily with a scar on his leg of a size that his hand could not cover.

The scar gave emphasis to Dr. Emery's argument. In 1912, Professor Wily formed the Gas Cannon Company and the carbide cannon was put into production.

In 1916, the name was changed to the Toy Cannon Works and then in 1924 the company became the Conestoga Company we know today.

James Hunter Wily, July 12, 1879 - January 3, 1962.

Through my research I have become acquainted with and impressed by Professor Wily. He is one of those specially gifted people who would excel at anything he tried.

Wily was a teacher, an inventor, a successful business man and he has left us with the legacy of a wonderful toy, the safe and sane celebrator, the BIG-BANG carbide cannon.

This restored 7F has flat wheels (no ribs) and a wheel type breech block.

Wily (far right) celebrating the Armistice with members of the Lehigh staff.

CHAPTER THREE

THE GAS CANNON COMPANY

The Gas Cannon is the first mass produced cannon we can attribute to Professor Wily's efforts. This iron cannon was produced in two forms, one using a glowing platinum wire for ignition and one using a spark for ignition. No advertising for these cannons has come to light but they were probably about one or two dollars when new.

Cover Illustration from the Gas Cannon Booklet.

The photo on the cover of a surviving instruction manual shows two small boys shooting down forts of blocks. Having a Gas Cannon, I became curious as to its battering power and made a hardwood projectile to test the cannon against walls of blocks. The effect was devastating. After a few well placed shots, the need was seen for heavier blocks. By any definition, the Gas Cannon with its machined one inch bore, is real artillery and should be fired with projectiles only on a range. Is this is how children played in 1912?

In 1915, the Artillery Game replaced the Gas Cannon. The first thing you will notice is the glass barrel. Yes, the iron barrel on the Gas Cannon has been replaced with a thick glass barrel for the Artillery Game. We can only speculate why this change was made.

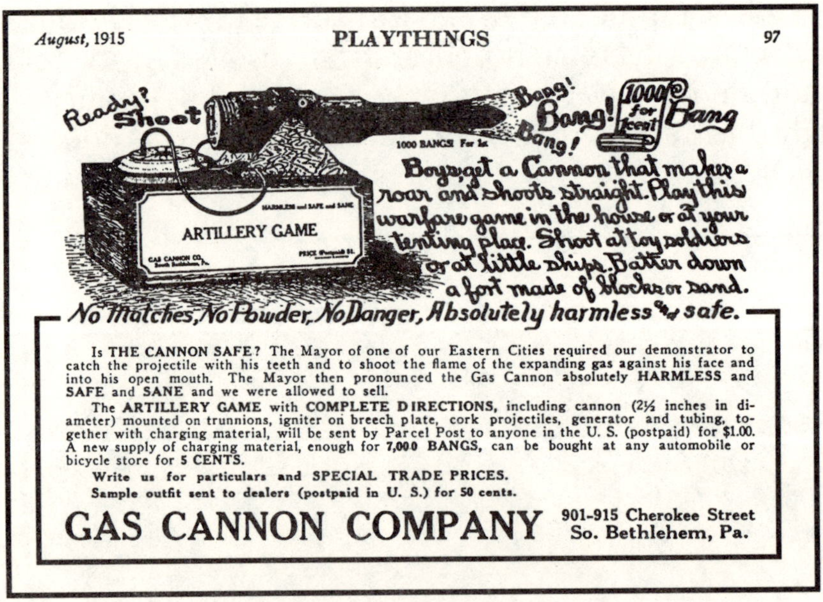

Artillery Game Ad. Playthings August 1915.

Was it for economic reasons? Was iron suddenly scarce because of the war in Europe? Did Wily think the flash of the explosion should be seen?

The Artillery Game used the same gas generator as the Gas Cannon. It used the time tested inverted vessel to both contain the gas and supply the pressure to move it to the gun via a rubber tube. The tube passes through a notch in the sheet metal mount where a wire spring acts as an on-off valve by pinching the tube shut. Ignition is provided by a wheel and flint spark device mounted in the breech cap that screws onto the cannon barrel like a lid screws onto a jar. This change to flint ignition is a major step in the evolution and eventual success of the toy.

Outside of the ignition, the gun is operated the same way as the Gas Cannon. The resulting vacuum from the explosion draws enough oxygen back into the barrel to mix with the acetylene for the next shot. The advertising of the day still approves of not only firing cannons in the house but using projectiles as well! Information indicates that the glass barreled cannons were made for only one year, 1915. Only 5000 glass cannons were made.

William Suddards Franklin, Professor of Physics.

In spite of the grand effect the transparent combustion chamber must have had when firing the guns, day or night, Wily recognized the adverse effect it must have had on sales. Visions of the glass tube shattering and putting eyes out for miles around must have prevented many a kid from getting a hold of the toy of his dreams.

The truth of the matter is that while an oxy-acetylene explosion produces a sharp crack, it has relatively little power and probably did not break any glass barrels.

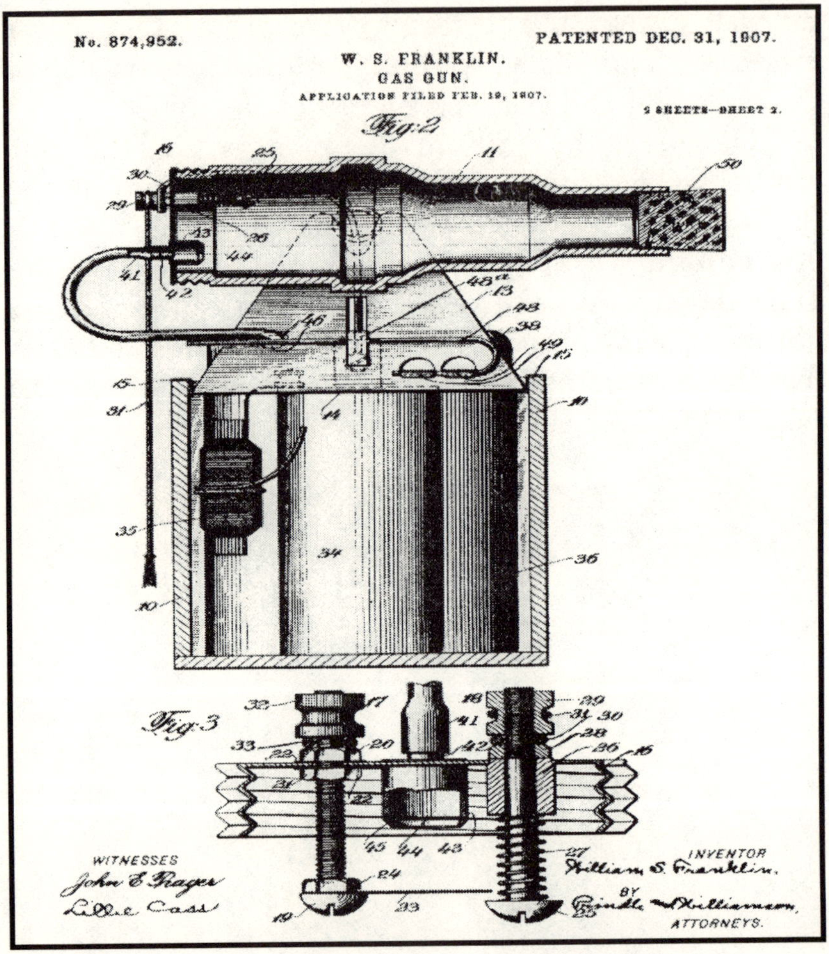

Page 1 Graphic from Franklin's Patent #874,952.

Nevertheless, glass is not iron and the casualty rate must have been high with cannons breaking for other reasons and very few have survived the years.

It is the close resemblance between the Artillery Game and a gas cannon patent granted in 1907 that compelled me to search for the connection. The only major variation between the two is the ignition system.

This patent is assigned to William Suddards Franklin who just happened to be a physics professor at Lehigh from 1903 to 1915. Franklin was surely one of Wily's teachers, maybe even his mentor. Perhaps they were good friends.

Franklin refers to his invention as a "...new and useful Improvement in Gas-Guns...". What gas guns could have predated Franklin's? Well, gas guns could not have predated carbide, could they? If so, what gas did they use and just when was carbide invented?

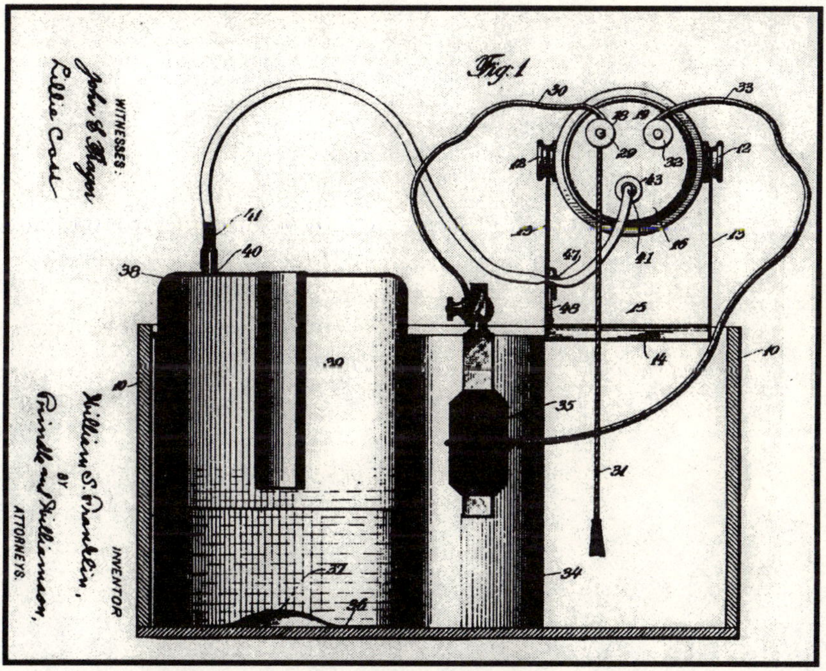

Page 2 Graphic from Franklin's Patent #874,952.

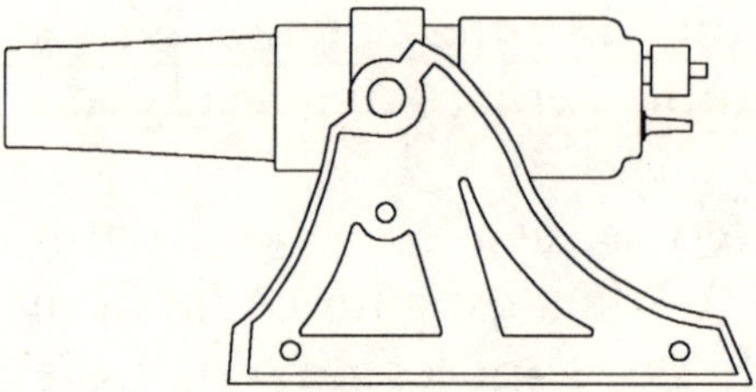

The Gas Cannon

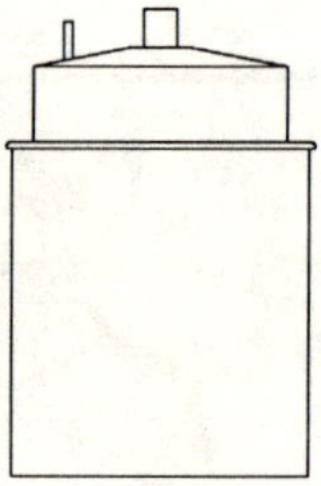

Both Cannons Used this Gas
Generator and Holder.

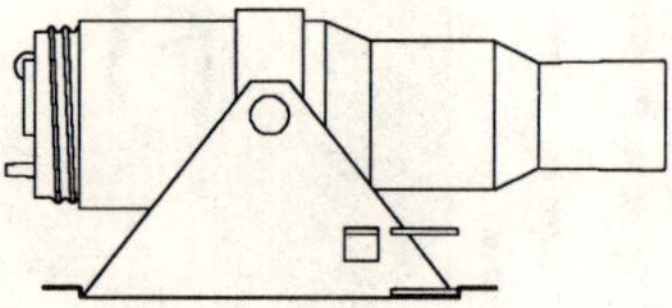

The Artillery Game

The Two Toys Marketed by the Gas Cannon Company, 1912 - 1915.

CHAPTER FOUR
ORIGINS

The Gun...

Patent #874,952 was issued on the last day of 1907 to

W.S.Franklin, somewhere in Wyoming.

William Suddards Franklin of Bethlehem, Pennsylvania. Franklin was born October 27, 1863 in Geary City, Kansas. He earned his bachelor's and masters's degrees at the University of Kansas in 1887 and in 1888, taking his doctorate at Cornell in 1901. He was an assistant professor of physics at the University of Kansas and went to Iowa State College to become a professor of physics and electrical engineer there.

In 1897, he went to Lehigh University in Bethlehem, Pennsylvania. In 1903, he was made professor and head of the physics department and remained until he resigned in July of 1915. It was in the physics department at Lehigh where Wily and Franklin met.

Wily graduated Lehigh in 1905 with the degree, E.E. (Electrical Engineer) so apparently he was one of Franklin's pupils. According to Lehigh, Wily was an instructor in the physics department from 1906 to 1909 when was made assistant professor, the post he occupied at Lehigh until 1920. From all of this it can be assumed that Franklin and Wily were closely associated at Lehigh.

Franklin's patent is for a carbide cannon and that was 1907. But accounts tell us in 1910 that Wily had a brass toy cannon of his own design in his office at his Lehigh lab where he was developing household refrigeration (word is that Westinghouse beat Wily to the patent office by a matter of hours).

From interviews with three of Franklin's grandchildren, the same story comes across. Apparently Wily was Franklin's assistant. The two men co-invented the cannon. When Franklin left Lehigh in 1915, he gave it (the cannon, the patent, the Gas Cannon Company?) to Wily. This story makes sense and is supported by other significant changes that happened during or shortly after 1915. Whether or not they had collaborated on the project, chances are both these men were influenced by experiments that began more than a century earlier.

History Lesson...

In 1777 Joseph Priestley, credited with discovering oxygen, was exploding gases in cannon by means of an electric spark. Alexandre Volta, who invented the means

Alxendre Volta

for making that spark (the volt is named after him), heard about this and went right out and began his own experiments with flammablc gasscs. Thc cnd rcsult was his electric pistol, as he called it, that used his electric spark to explode l'air inflammable, swamp gas, methane and the like.

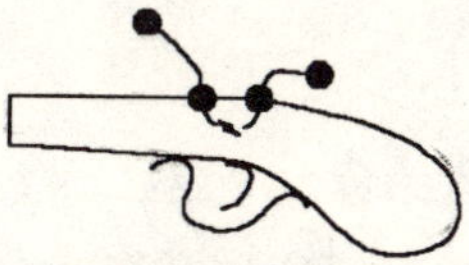

The Electric Pistol.

Carbide cannons are used to this day to demonstrate explosive atmospheres and Volta's pistol or some variation of it was most likely used down through the years initially for testing the air and then for demonstrations. It is not unlikely that Franklin and Wily were subjected to these demonstrations as students and perhaps the roots of the carbide cannon lie in the need to demonstrate a gas explosion with less fuss than tapping a burner into a bean can and tossing in a match.

It is not a sure thing, but a couple of physics professors who were electrical engineers certainly must have studied Volta and might have gotten an idea from the electric pistol, which was, by the way, made of glass.

154 PREMIERE

faire des épreuves multipliées, & à modifier l'appa-reil, en ſuivant la meme conſtruction. J'en ai fait faire en verre, & l'expérience à cauſé autant de plai-ſir que de ſurpriſe anx ſpectateurs qui voyoient au travers du verre, & l'air pur qui le rempliſſoit, & la flamme de l'exploſion.

Quoique donc dans les premieres conſtructions, dans lesquelles on fait jouer un piſton, la charge

"I have had it done in glass and the experiment caused so much more pleasure than surprise in the spectators watching..." From Lettres De Mr. Alexandre Volta

The Gas...

Acetylene was know to exist as early as 1837 and a few patents for barium carbide exist. In 1893, Thomas L. Willson was granted U.S. patent #492,377 for "Electric Reduction of Refractory Metallic compounds". Of the many uses for Willson's process the production of calcium carbide held the best promise of financial success and was therefore specifically mentioned in the patent.

Willson initiated the commercial development of calcium carbide in America by selling the rights to

> the treatment of refractory compounds or ores of metals, not necessarily for the production of the metals themselves, but for the production of other compounds thereof. For example, I have already employed it for reducing calcium oxide and producing calcium carbide.
>
> I claim as my invention the following de-

From Willsons Patent, No. 442,601.

interests that were to become the Electro-Gas Company. In 1898, the name was changed to the Union Carbide Company and was until recently the world's largest producer of calcium carbide.

Fire in the hole...

About the same time carbide became available, misch metal was discovered in Germany. Misch metal is pyromorphic; it makes sparks when scratched. BIG-BANG spark plugs are misch metal and so are lighter flints. Misch metal is the active ingredient in all sparking toys. The material is called misch metal because it is a combination of miscellaneous rare earth metals.

Misch metal is roughly 50% Cerium, 25% Lantha-

BIG-BANG Spark Plug Package.

num, 15% Neodymium, 6% Praseodymium and 4% miscellaneous compounds. The exact alloy of the flint depends on the end use, but for the scope of this text we will use 80% misch metal and 18% iron. The remaining 2% is made up of magnesium and zinc that enhance the manufacturing process which is generally extrusion. The resulting alloy is known as Ferrocerium.

BIG-BANG "spark plugs" were once supplied by the Ronson Corporation, but are no longer produced in the United States.

Rare Earth elements are hydrophoric, that is they absorb hydrogen, which is what eventually leads to their deterioration and the iron in flints will oxidize causing them to crumble. I believed this is why flints are painted; it is not, the finish is only a color code.

The Winning Combination...

On November 4, 1915, Professor Wily applied to the patent office with his new design. The great innovation in Wily's cannon is that for the first time we see the tremendous simplification brought about by moving the gas generator to the inside of the cannon.

Generating the acetylene inside the cannon in a timely fashion is only made possible by using pulverized

Ser. No. 614,183. James H. Wily, doing business as The Conestoga Company, Bethlehem, Pa. Filed May 21, 1951.

BANGSITE

For Ammunition for Toy Cannon and Fire Arms. Claims use since Dec. 1, 1917.

Trademark From The Official Gazette.

carbide instead of the larger lumps commonly supplied for use in lamps and welding. Wily called his powdered carbide Bangsite and registered the trademark in 1917.

The breech block of the cannon is fitted with a small spoon used to measure the carbide. With the spoon loaded up with Bangsite, it is put into the breech of the

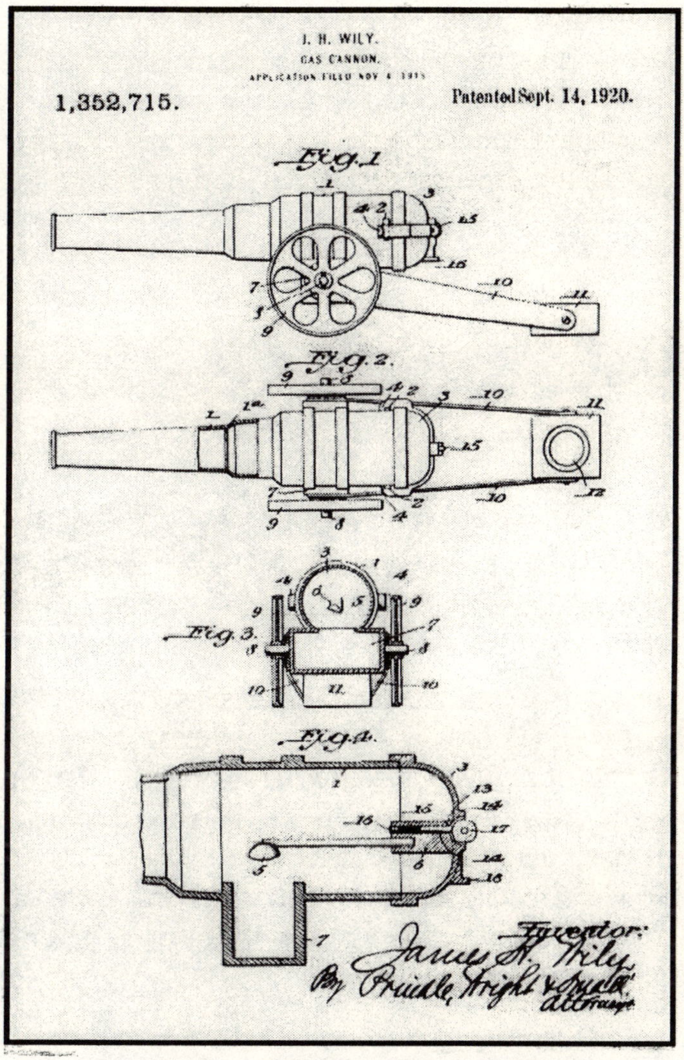

Wily's First (And Most Important) Patent.

gun. The quarter turn required to lock the breech block in place rotates the spoon, dumping its contents into the water sump below where the reaction takes place and in just a couple of seconds, the acetylene is produced.

The acetylene mixes with the air in the cannon chamber forming a localized explosive atmosphere. The misch metal spark ignites the gases that burn almost instantaneously producing the desired report.

The four things leading to the success of the Big-Bang cannon are; 1) Bangsite that makes possible 2) metered gas generation without an external generator 3) flint spark ignition that eliminates external batteries and matches

Perfection and Simplicity, the BIG-BANG Cannon.

and 4) the necessity of removing the breech to reload causes the cannon to be ventilated, thus replacing the oxygen used up during firing.

Now a simple, safe, and self-contained toy of wondrous noise making capacity was about to be given to the boys of the world.

CHAPTER FIVE

THE TOY CANNON WORKS

Cannon production started in a two car garage on Clewell Street in Fountain Hill, PA then moved to larger quarters on Cherokee Street while still producing the Artillery Game.

Professor Wily applied for his aforementioned patent November 4, 1915, but it was not granted until 5 years later on September 14, 1920. The delay, however, did not slow down the Professor one bit.

Glass Barreled Demonstrator, from the Conestoga Collection.

The first toys made to incorporate Wily's innovations are the three cannons we see advertised in *Playthings* of July 1916, the 11D, the 11F and the 16F. This was the debut of the first all iron cannons as well as the name BIG-BANG which was trademarked the following year.

The ad illustrates the 11F and the 11D. The 16F is

mentioned as though it was added in on short notice. The following year, 1917, advertisements refer to "..three sizes- 7, 11, and 16-inch barrels. 5 models.." and one must assume that the latest additions were the 7F and 7D.

One distinguishing feature of BIG-BANGS is that they all had an ammunition compartment. The field artillery had a dandy little chest at the end of the drags. The capacity of the magazine on the 16F could swallow a whole tube of Bangsite. The 11D barrel is unique among BIG-BANGS in that its magazine is integral with the water sump. This casting required two cores and because of this, it was a more difficult cannon to produce.

Ignition is provided by a wheel and flint mounted in the die-cast breech block. The block has two lugs that engaged two lugs on the cannon breech. The cannon's lugs are tapered and as you turn the breech block, it tightens down against the breech face. One lug on the breech block is much thinner than the other and over tightening causes it to break off and many of them did.

The early 1917 ads show the 11" models with the words BIG-BANG on the larger diameter of the cannon barrel, but I have never seen such an example.

I have seven 7" BIG-BANGS, but only one has BIG-BANG in one side and MODEL7 in the other. Fine detail in castings compounds the problems of the foundry men and the wording was dropped from the Model 7 and may never have been used on the other sizes.

The pistol was first produced around 1922. It is all die-cast white metal. The patent shows that the gun could be separated into two halves for cleaning, but in fact the production pistols were riveted tight.

The butt of the pistol housed the magazine which has a hinged lid with a spring that held it open. The same spring also held it closed. When it was open a mere touch caused it to snap closed. A lot of thought went into the pistol design.

July, 1916 PLAYTHINGS 15

"BIG-BANG"

Harmless, and Safe and Sane
No Matches-No Powder-No Danger

The Junior Defense "BIG-BANG" consists of an 11-inch tilting cannon mounted on a heavy metal base, as shown in the picture. This base is black-enameled as well as the ammunition case which is a part of the support of the cannon. The color of the breech-plate is battleship-gray. This cannon is intended for all ages and can be operated with safety by a child of seven. The cannon body itself is 11 inches long, and the total length from the muzzle to the rear end of the base is 12¾ inches. The complete outfit is metal and weighs 3½ pounds. Shipping Weight, 4 pounds.

Model 11 DB—Junior Defense Black Enameled Cannon

"BIG-BANG"

Harmless and Safe and Sane
No Matches-
No Powder-No Danger

The Junior Field "BIG-BANG" consists of an 11-inch tilting cannon mounted on red-enameled wheels and has a black ammunition case attached at the end of the black-enameled drag beams. The color of the breech-plate is battleship-gray. This cannon is intended for all ages and can be operated with safety by a child of seven. The cannon body itself is 11 inches long, and the total length is 16 inches from the muzzle to the ammunition case at the rear. The complete outfit is metal and weighs 4 pounds. Shipping Weight, 4½ pounds.

Model 11 FB—Junior Field Black Enameled Cannon

Also Model 16 F. B.—Major Field Black Enameled Cannon

A 16-inch tilting cannon with wheels, same finish as Model 11 F.B. This cannon is intended for older ones, but can be operated with safety by a child of seven. The cannon body itself is 16 inches long, and the total length is **23 inches** from the muzzle to the ammunition case at the rear. The complete outfit is metal and weighs 6¾ pounds. Shipping Weight, 7½ pounds.

The Owens-Kreiser Co.
29-33 East 19th Street New York

1916 BIG-BANG AD.

A short dam inside the gun at the barrel keeps enough water in even when the pistol is holstered; a small drain plug facilitates cleaning. The flint and plunger were surrounded by a fine screen that keep water from splashing onto them. One of Wily's nephews writes; "I remember having a pistol.... It was an engineering masterpiece. ... it could be loaded, placed in the holster, and fired later, although not too much later."

One of the drawbacks of the pistol is the way the trigger engages the firing mechanism in the breech block. If you try to rotate the breech while the trigger is still engaged, you can break off the part that pushes the plunger. In addition, if you pull the trigger too hard, the upper part will break.

My pistol came from Charles Best, the cap gun expert and author of Cast Iron Toy Pistols, 1870-1940, and he advised me never to shoot mine. I never have, but if I had two pistols....

In 1923 wheels were added to the 11D and it became a new model, the 10W, Heavy Artillery. Also introduced at that time is the plunger type ignition.

The most obvious improvement in the new breech block is that both lugs are the same size. Less apparent is the flint adjusting screw now on the outside of the cannon

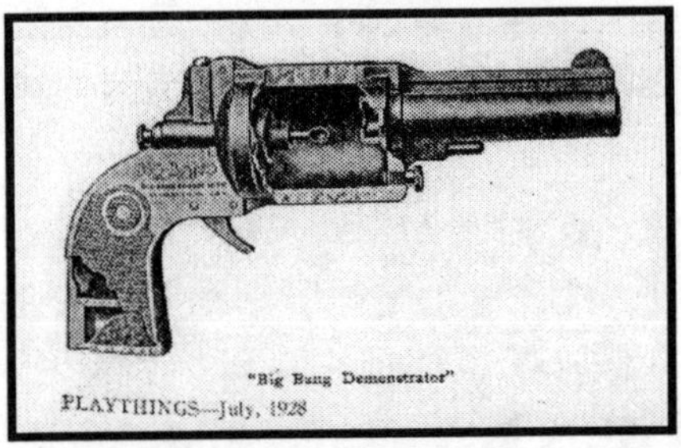

BIG-BANG Pistol demonstrator.

when the breech block is in place. The inside of the cannon is a humid place and powder spoons rust away and the adjusting screw in the old wheel breech blocks must have seized up regularly.

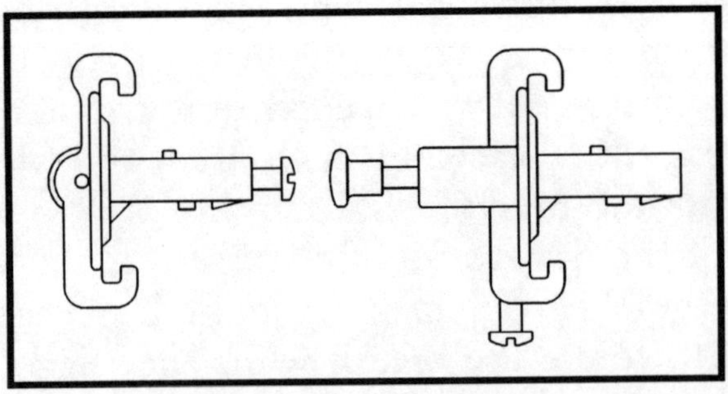

Wheelie (left) and Plunger (right) Breech Blocks.

The 10W was introduced with the now rare Tear-Drop Wheels.

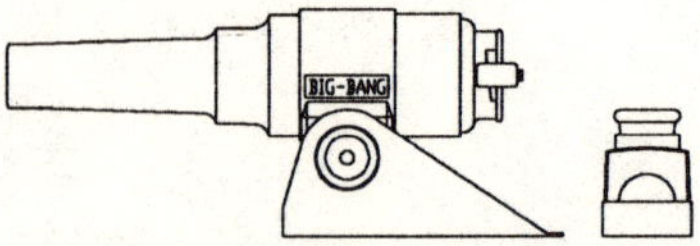

7D - Junior Defense ($1.25)

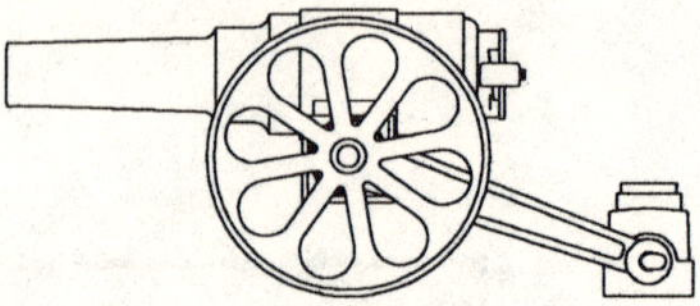

7F - Junior Field Cannon ($1.75)

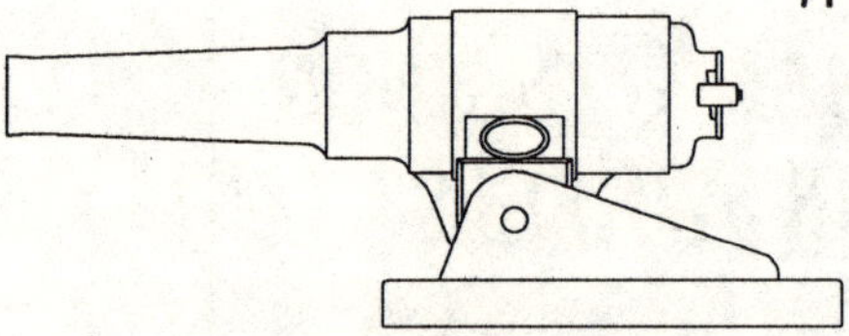

11D - Major Defense ($2.50)

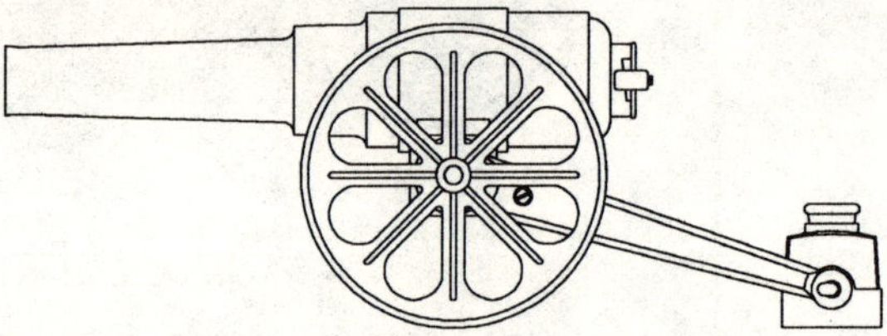

11F - Major Field Cannon ($3.50)

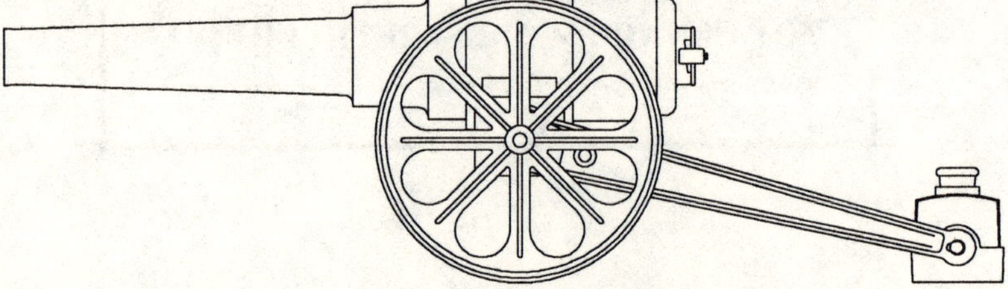

16F - Siege Field Gun ($5.00)

BIG-BANGS you could buy in 1917 from the Toy Cannon Works. (new prices)

CHAPTER SIX

THE CONESTOGA COMPANY

Wily's marketing strategy was aimed in two directions; at the child for how much fun a BIG-BANG promised and at the parent for the inherent safety of the carbide cannon.

In the first ad for the Artillery Game, we see the words that are used to this day; SAFE and SANE. Then in 1918, the "Kid" first appeared. The photo shows the boy firing a BIG-BANG 16F with his left hand in the muzzle blast and the caption is; "Don't hurt a bit". We haven't been able to determine who the kid is. It is not Wily's son, perhaps one of Franklin's?

The Kid...

Bangsite was trademarked December 1, 1917 and shows up in the BIG-BANG *Playthings* December ad of that year. Unlike black powder, commonly referred to as powder, Bangsite can not be ignited by flame nor can it be set off by percussion. Bad enough that fireworks and powder were dangerous in themselves; these things required matches at a time when buildings burned quicker and fire equipment was largely horse drawn. Keeping matches out of children's hands was a big parental concern.

The reason carbide was safe is that there is nothing that will burn until it is combined with water. The resulting reaction takes the carbon from the carbide and hydrogen from the water and forms the compound H_2C_2, acetylene. This mixes with the air in the cannon chamber to produce an explosive atmosphere. Too much carbide and you get a gas rich mixture; not having enough oxygen, it produces an oily flame with a weak report. Not enough carbide and you get no pop at all. The volume of the cannon exactly determines the amount of material that can be exploded.

"An under charge or over charge only means a weaker report. Bangsite cannot be lighted with a match and will not explode when hit with a hammer." These words appeared in many BIG-BANG ads.

During the Great War, Wily used the powder shortage and fireworks' laws to his advantage admonishing buyers to "obey the law" in his advertisements and sales must have been encouraging. During the 1920's, ten new models were brought out.

The pistol marks the first instance of the "embodiment in many different forms" of Wily's patent. The pistols are marked: BIG-BANG CANNON WORKS. The molds were not changed when the company became the Conestoga Company.

In 1923, a *Playthings* ad shows (for the first time) the

10W with the "new plunger-type breech block". Going by this, we can assume that the wheel-type breech blocks were by that time discontinued and they should be dated no later than 1923. By the same token, the plunger-type ignition should be dated no earlier than 1923, in spite of the Sept. 1920 patent date molded in them.

In 1924, the company moved to Conestoga St. and

The Conestoga Letterhead.

Prospect Ave. in Bethlehem, Pa. and incorporated as the Conestoga Company. You would think that this is where Wily got the Conestoga name from. In fact, Conestoga St. was a semi-private road at the time and Wily didn't even know it had a name. The Conestoga Pike (Pa. 401) passed near Wily's boyhood home in Chester County and it was the pike that gave the company the name. No, the street was not named for the company either. A map dated 1886 reprinted in Bethlehem Of Pennsylvania-The Golden Years, clearly shows Conestoga Street.

October, 1924 finds the Navy Gun Boat featured in ads placed by the then new Conestoga Company. Like the pistol, the Navy Gun Boat is another embodiment of the patent in a shape other than that of cannon. The boat is cast iron and rides on four wooden wheels. The words "BIG-BANG" are cast into the foredeck, but the ad is misleading as "CONESTOGA" is not at all in the casting.

Loose pieces include the breech block, two steel

turrets that serve as magazine covers, the funnel (smoke stack) and flagpole with flag. This is one of my neatest

Model 9B, Navy Gun Boat.

cannons. The twin barrels are more like enlarged hawse pipes and they are slightly angled out and down so that this piece "snorts" when fired!

In 1926, the first 5T tank was introduced. The big news here is that we see for the first time the bayonet breech block. The turret is die-cast white metal and the barrel is a steel tube pressed in with a brass ring at the muzzle. This assembly is then put into the body which is made of wood with tin tracks tacked on. The ads say you can fire it by stepping on it. Repeating this practice surely caused the collapse of many a turret.

Going through the old magazines in the New York Public Library, one begins to sense technology and history as it unfolded. Through the teens and 20's electrification progressed and electric toys appeared in greater numbers.

So, it is not unusual to see the tremendous surge in aviation and *air-o-plane* toys ignited by Lindbergh's famous solo. All the airplane toys of the day resembled the Spirit of St. Louis in that none had wind screens; Conestoga's Bombing Plane was no different.

The 11P Bombing Plane has to rank as one of the oddest toys ever made. Is it a cannon? No. Is it a plane? Well sort of. It is too heavy (4 1/2 lbs.) even for a boy to run around with it held in the air, and I find it impossible

The Baby of the BIG-BANG family, Model 5T, Army Tank.

to even imagine it in flight! But, it does make noise! And it does spin the propeller with every shot. Of all my "cannons", the airplane rates as the most novel.

Also introduced in 1929, at the same time as the Bombing Plane, is the venerable 6F. The 6F is the first to use the sheet-metal breech plate for the bayonet breech block and is possibly the smallest practical carbide cannon ever made. With the exception of the World War II years, the 6F has been in continuous production from 1929 and is still being made today. It is estimated over five million have been produced.

Due to the small size difference between the 6F and 7F, I first believed 1929 was when the 7F and 11F were replaced. As more information came to light, my assumption proved false. The 12F is mentioned by name as early

ARTILLERY FIELD CANNON—Continued

This new model is mounted on two red wheels. The ammunition case is in the rear end of the heavy drag beam.

Catalogue number is:

6F—$1.00

Model 6F—LIGHT FIELD GUN

Finished in black gun-metal—semi-gloss.
Length of non-tilting cannon body—6 inches.
Length end of muzzle to end of drag—9 inches.
One in a box. Weight, 2¼ lbs. Price, $1.00

Introduced in 1929, The 6F is still in production today.

as December 1925 and the 8F was first noticed in 1924. Apparently the larger sizes came out in 1923 with the new 10W.

The Bombing Plane.

10W ($3.00)

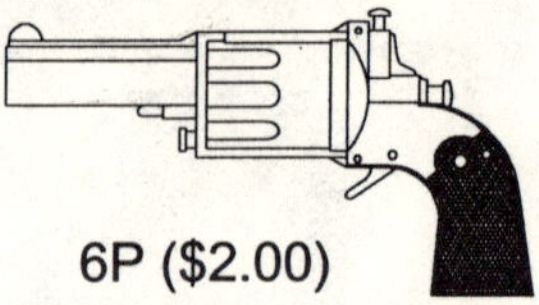

6P ($2.00)

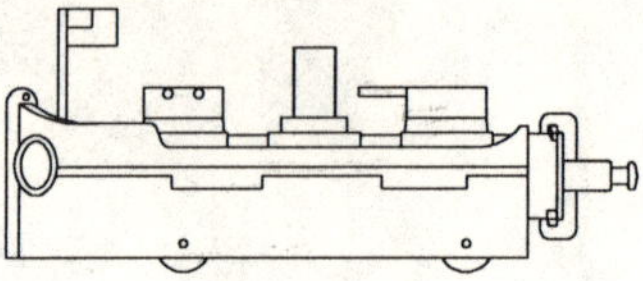

9B ($2.00)

8F ($2.25)

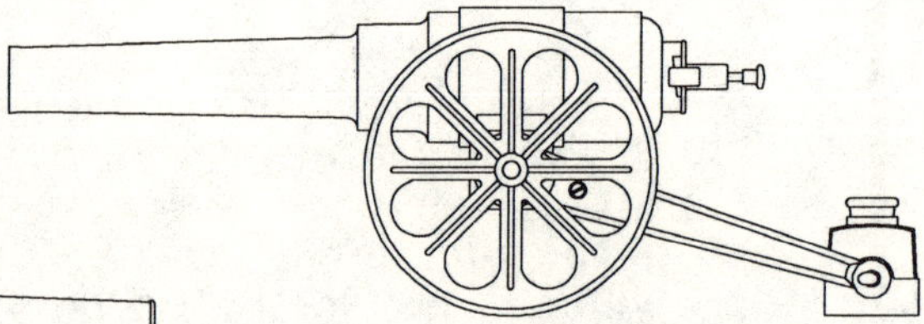

12F ($3.75)

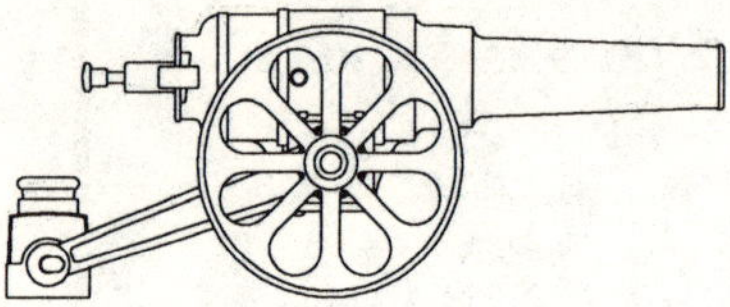

8FR ($2.50)

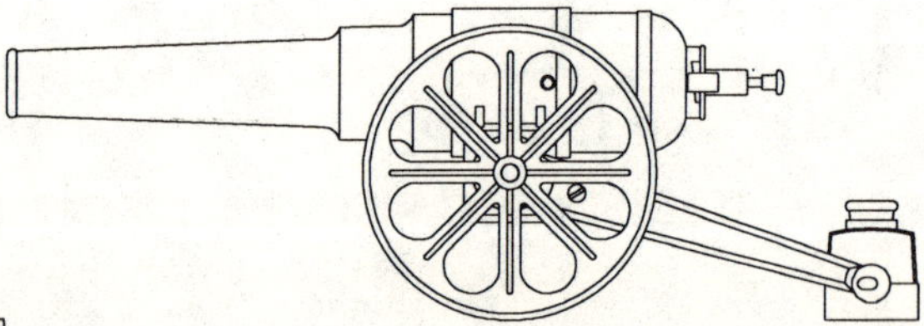

12FR (price unknown)

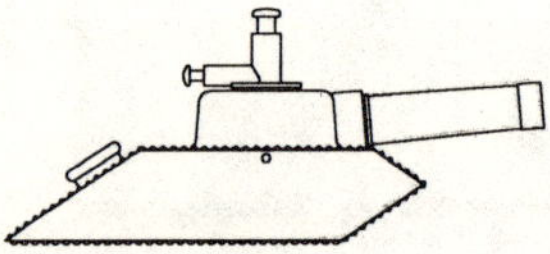

5T ($1.00)

11P ($3.50)

6F ($1.50)

Wily brought out ten new numbers during the Roaring Twenties. (new prices)

CHAPTER SEVEN

THE DEPRESSION

With the stock market collapse in 1929, the country started its slide into depression. Many firms were ruined outright, but others had the resources to carry on hoping things would turn around soon. The Conestoga Company was one of them.

About 1930, the original airplane design was replaced by the more robust over & under version. The earlier design was inferior in that the very vulnerable propeller and shaft were die-cast white metal; not a material for abuse.

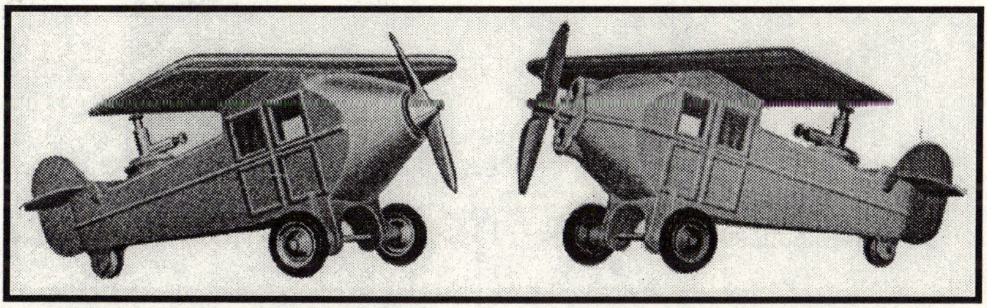

Early Die-Cast Nose *Common Over & Under*

The new version, on the other hand, got rid of the tubular steel barrel that went from the nose to the combustion chamber. In its place were the two smaller over & under ports integral with the main casting.

The propeller shaft is brass and is held in place with a small cotter pin. The propeller itself is two pieces of stamped steel, spot welded together.

Of the two airplanes, the over & under is the more common. The earlier version was grey and black, while most over & unders were painted cream and green, but there are some cream and maroon ones out there.

Wily hoped to make the company stronger by diver-

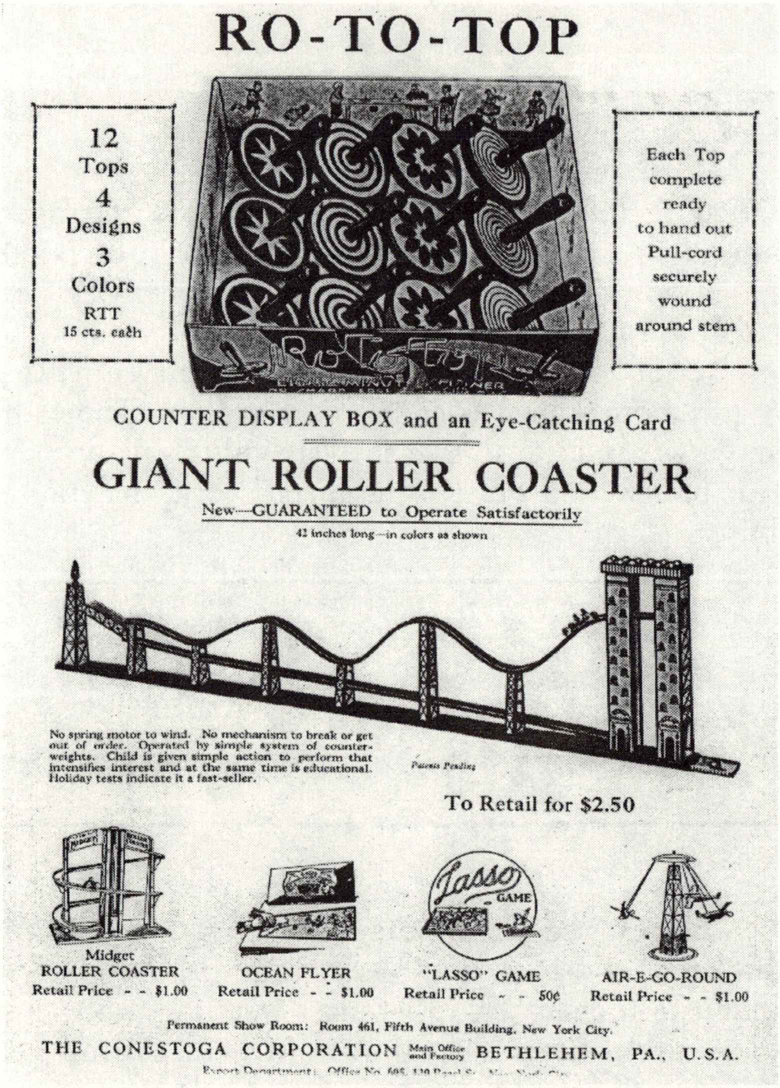

Wily wanted Conestoga to be more than just a cannon company.

sifying and 1929 marked an expansion of non-cannon toys for Conestoga. The heavy die-cast RO-TO-TOP, first introduced about 1924, was redesigned in iron and given flashy colors.

In 1930, we see the Giant Roller Coaster advertised in *Playthings,* along with the Air-E-Go Round, the Ocean Flyer, the Midget Roller Coaster and finally Wily's patented New Giant Roller Coaster.

Not to leave anything out, 1931 saw the Lasso Game and the Two-Car Racer. Conestoga manufactured many of these non-cannon toys, but some were made by others and marketed by Wily. There was an Air-E-Go Round advertised in *Antique Toy World*, but it was already sold when I called and the dealer told me it was marked "REEVES".

Peak unemployment forced deep price cuts.

In 1933, with unemployment at a peak, cannon prices were slashed to stimulate sagging sales. You could have had an airplane, mint-in-box, for 95 cents!

In 1935, Conestoga redesigned it's entire line and discontinued the old models. The little 6F was the only model that survived the purge.

The new models featured the automatic charger and all cannons used the sheet-metal breach cap with the bayonet breech block. Two basic gun sizes were introduced that are still made today in several configurations. 15FC and smaller 10FC were field pieces and the 15AC was an anti-aircraft pattern on an iron swivel base. The charger lid for the 10FC is also marked for the 10AC and it would seem that a smaller AA gun may have been thought of, but there is no evidence of one ever being produced.

The Conestoga Field Glass featured a unique snap-up snap-down lens cover.

Also introduced in 1935 were the field glasses that went on to become official Boy Scout issue. No good artillery man would be caught without them. Conestoga manufactured the Model FG-66 field glasses into the mid to late 50's.

By this time in my research, I was confident that all the Conestoga cannons were accounted for. Now that the current models have been introduced, my only remaining interest was when the Motor Tank of my childhood and the rubber-tired MM series was added to the line.

MARCH, 1941—PLAYTHINGS

Big-Bang Motor Tank

"BIG-BANG" CELEBRATORS

The Conestoga Corp. will be on hand at the Hotel McAlpin during the Toy Fair with their brand new "Big-Bang" Motor Tank, a very formidable looking miniature tank that actually fires harmless charges of "Bangsite." In addition, the complete line, including cannons of all types and a new line of mulfti-colored spinning tops, will be shown by J. H. Wily.

Playthings New Products Featured the 5T Motor Tank.

I was surprised to find the model 5T Motor Tank was introduced in March 1941. Because it has rubber tires, I had previously thought that this one was brought out with the rest of the rubber tired MM series. It uses the same turret, barrel and breech block as the earlier Army Tank. Instead of a wooden body, the gun is now supported by an iron hull carried on four rubber tires. The magazine is at the rear as with the Army Tank, but it is the shallow dish type that was used on the Gun Boat. The magazine cover is also borrowed from the boat.

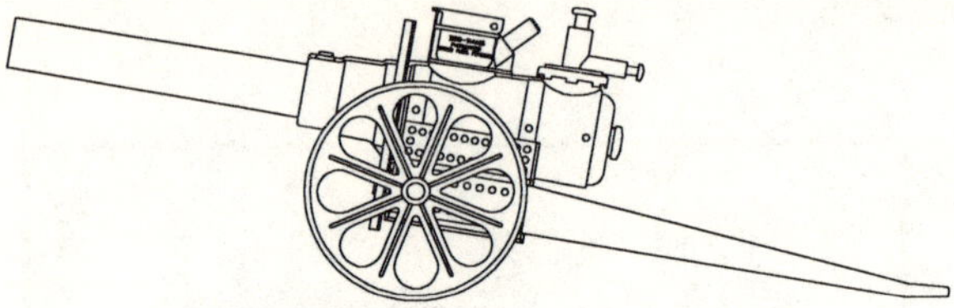

10FC ($2.50)

15FC ($3.00)

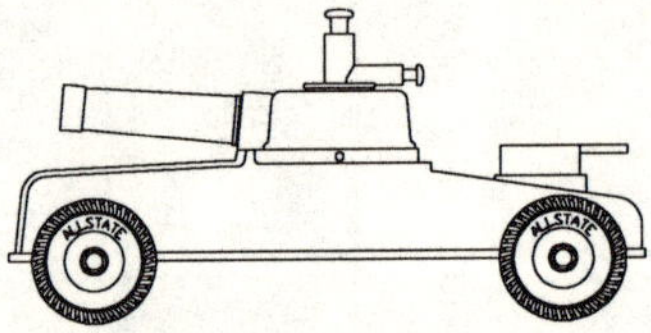

5T ($2.50)

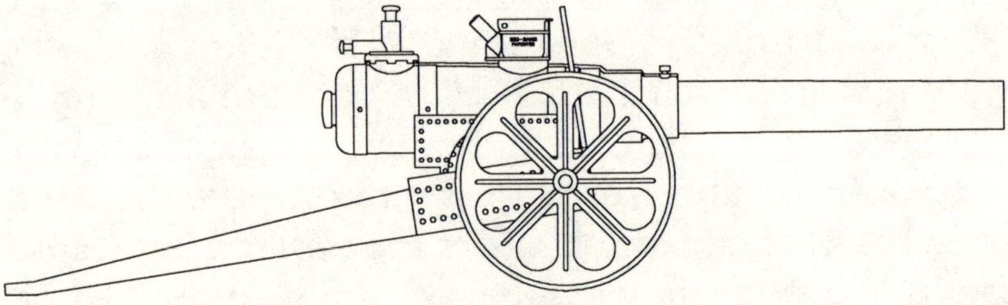

115FC ($3.50)

The last BIG-BANGS to be introduced by Wily. (new prices)

CHAPTER EIGHT
BRUNO, GOMBOTZ & SPINOSA

Production of toy cannons was suspended during the war years as the country's resources were diverted to more pressing needs, but one could still get Bangsite and spark plugs. Right after the war, the lead used for Bangsite tubes was in short supply and the tubes were not available. For a couple of years, Bangsite was put up in foil packets, a few of which survive today in David Spinosa's collection.

Assorted Bangsite Packages.

In 1951, Wily was incapacitated after being struck by a train and in 1952 the Conestoga plant was badly damaged by fire and the company lay idle. In 1955, Wily sold Conestoga to the Miller brothers, Frank and Robert. That is when Joseph Gombotz got a call asking if he would be interested in helping to start production of the BIG-BANG cannon.

Joseph Gombotz began working at Conestoga "about 1946". He returned to Behtlehem Steel in 1950 when the Korean War broke out. He did not know the Millers, but he did accept their offer. The Millers owned a new car dealership and could not spend a lot of time getting Conestoga back together, so along with Gombotz, George Bruno was picked to help manage the company.

Several years later Gombotz and Bruno purchased Robert Miller's share of the company and not long after that Frank Miller's share as well. Bruno died in 1976 and Gombotz became the sole owner.

It must have been a tough job getting Conestoga back in order. Gombotz proudly told me "it was a lot of hard work, but we did it". Imagine the problems they faced. Tooling, drawings and records destroyed by fire. Probably the casting patterns were safe at the foundry, but who knows what was lost when the plant burned. In spite of the difficulties, Conestoga rose up to reclaim the niche it had occupied for half a century.

Realizing that the toy-buying public was not overly influenced by tradition and nostalgia, the Millers wanted something new and a young draftsman came up with some ideas. These became the rubber-tired MM series introduced in March, 1958; basically, the same three field pieces, but with a face-lift provided by new sheet metal and rubber tires for that modern look.

The 6F was fitted with two rubber wheels and renamed the 60MM. The 10" and 15" barrels lost their shields and gained recoil shock absorbers. The four tires mounted dual on one axle for the 105MM and the eight tires mounted dual on two axles for the 155MM gave the guns the look of modern artillery made familiar to everyone by WWII.

While Gombotz owned the company, sales were

The 155MM was patterned after the lines of the U.S. Army's 155MM and 8" Howitzer. This 8" Howitzer is in front of Town Hall, Warren, NJ.

about evenly divided between the iron wheel and the rubber-tired versions. David Spinosa tells me that today the iron wheel models out-sell their MM counterparts at a ratio of about five to one.

Flea markets tend to offer a greater number of the rubber wheeled cannons. Although dealers often attempt to get the same price for both styles of cannons, due in part no doubt to the fact that both styles are offered new at the same price, the greater appeal of the iron wheel style means these cannons are in short supply. A 15FC often fetches $50 while a 155MM at $45 is generally overpriced.

Some time after 1957, the 5T and the 15AC were retired. The last ad I have showing them is dated September, 1957. Joseph Gombotz showed me a photo of Conestoga's setup at a trade show. Together in that photo, along with all the cannons that are made today, is the 6F Civil War set and the Motor Tank and the 15AC. Even though they were no longer advertised, the tank and the anti-aircraft models were probably available new from Conestoga into the early 60's.

In 1978, Ercole Spinosa was looking at business properties. One of the buildings he looked at was on Geopp St. in Bethlehem, where Conestoga was then located. This is where he met Joseph Gombotz and discovered the cannon company was for sale. Spinosa decided BIG-BANG was a good investment. Gombotz sold the business to Spinosa and retired, acting today in an advisory capacity to the current owners.

Today, the BIG-BANG torch is carried by Ercole's son David. Under David's guidance, Conestoga has enjoyed several years of steady growth. David is full of energy and enthusiasm for the cannons and is aware of the historic significance of the toy. "When we first bought the company, I went through all the old files and saved these old advertisements, like the one I sent to you, and that's where I found the foil Bangsite packages", David told me. He also confided that he wished he had the time to research and document the BIG-BANG as I was doing.

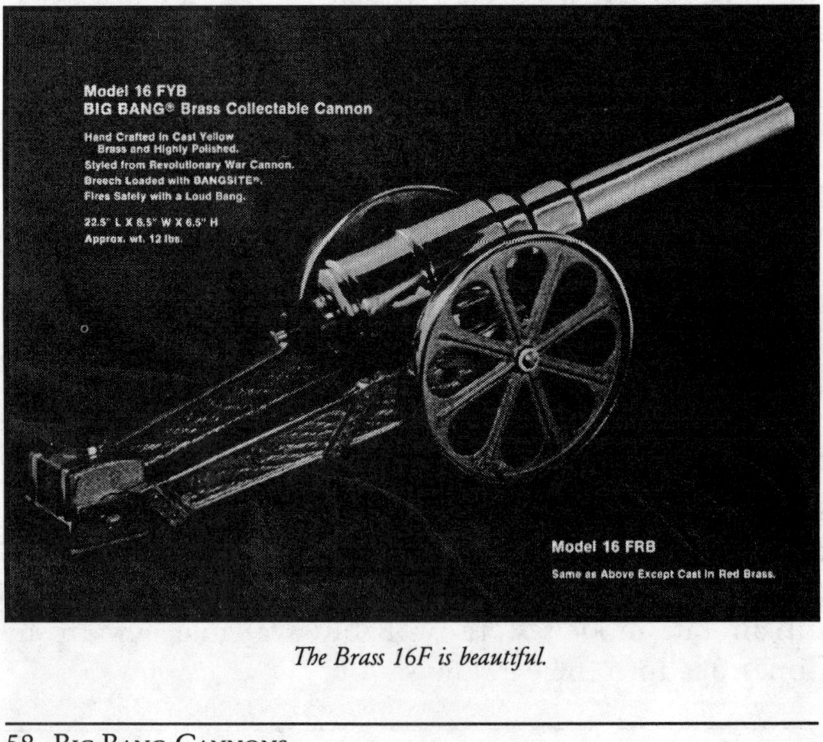

The Brass 16F is beautiful.

Shortly after buying Conestoga, Spinosa began a limited production of all brass replicas of the 16F and the 7F (8FYB). These cannons are polished to a mirror-like luster and are most impressive pieces. Originally the 16F was available in both red (16FRB) and yellow (16FRB) brass, but only the yellow version was available when Vincentine gave me one for Christmas in 1991. The 8FYB uses the pattern for the early 7F that has BIG-BANG and MODEL7 molded in the barrel. The 16FYB uses the replica white-metal breech block, but the 8FYB has a brass screw-in breech block with ignition via touch hole.

One notable change in the brass 16F's is the drags. The original drags were utilitarian, but the brass ones have an interesting design consisting of straps with rivets and rings, all on top of a wood grain pattern.

As we go to press, David Spinosa tells me that the red brass 16F will be re-issued. Perhaps by the time you read this, it will be available. Along with the 16FRB, David hinted at perhaps re-issuing the Gun Boat and even a reproduction of the beautiful multi-color BIG-BANG tin trade sign of the 1920's. The original sign is so rare and desirable that it can fetch up to fifteen hundred dollars in good condition. This is well out of the reach of most collectors like myself and a reasonably priced repro would be welcome indeed.

BIG-BANG tin trade sign. Caption in circle reads; "Harmless as a pop gun."

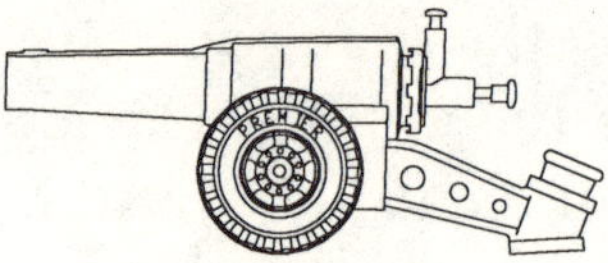

60MM ($3.95)

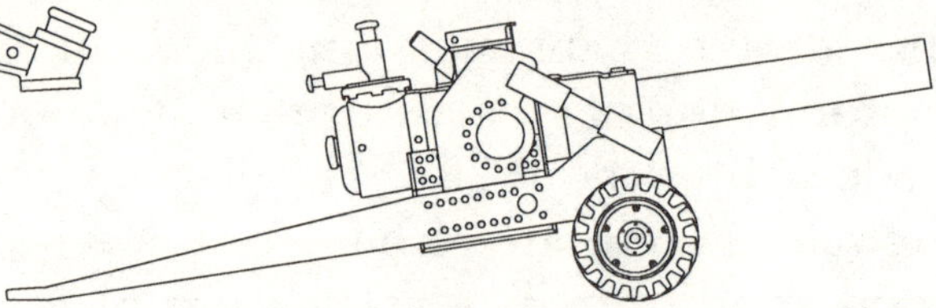

105MM ($9.95)

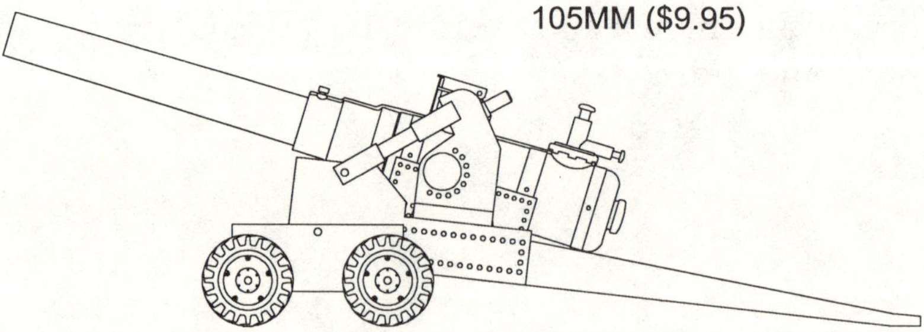

155MM ($14.95)

The MM series was introduced in 1958 and is still produced today.
(prices when introduced)

CHAPTER NINE
THE G-GUN

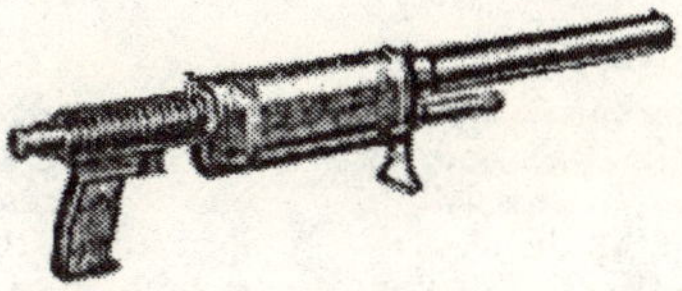

In January, 1992, I made my third trip to the New York Public Library Annex. My records show research started that day with Playthings, April 1930.

My research marched through the 30's turning up no new cannon products, although the Conestoga tin-litho toys appeared during this time span. The ads did not vary much and mostly served to confirm that Conestoga was still making a variety of toy cannons and celebrators.

The 1935 volumes were not available that day, but I already had a page from them that David Spinosa supplied showing the introduction of the charger models. I was ready to go home and not even look at the 1936 volumes which had been brought up. I can't remember what changed my mind, but I decided to go through 1936 anyway.

Have you ever been at a point when you thought you had it all down, you thought you knew it all, and there were no new discoveries to be made? I was at that point. All the old models were accounted for, the charger models were introduced in 1935, the motor tank and the MM series were known (but not dated), there just were not any more BIG-BANGS. Just when I thought I knew it all, there, on page 240 of the April issue of *Playthings*, was the Conestoga G-Gun.

I sat there stunned, staring at the page. Was this some

240 PLAYTHINGS

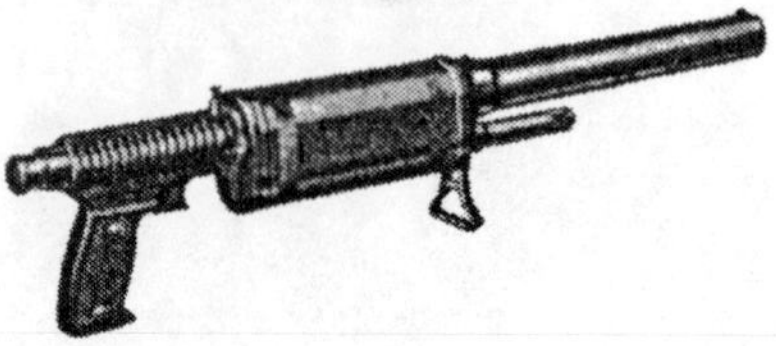

NEW BIG-BANG GUNS

The Conestoga Corporation of Bethlehem, Penna., announces that an entirely new item—The Big-Bang G-Gun will be shown for the first time at the American Toy Fair in the Hotel McAlpin, room 421. In addition to this new item the other Stream-Lined Automatic Big-Bang Safe-Celebrators include the model 6F Light Field Gun, model 10FC Junior Field Cannon, model 15FC Major Field Cannon and model 15AC Anti-Aircraft Gun. The new guns are reproductions of full size army field guns and are finished in olive-drab exactly as are the actual U. S. Army guns. These new models are equipped with a Charger and Ignitor. The Charger is located on top of the gun-body near the breech. It is a covered metal receptacle which holds enough Bangsite for about 50 shots. There is also a spring-operated plunger: one push on the charger plunger loads the gun with just the proper amount of Bangsite to make the loudest possible "Bang." The Plunger measures the charge automatically, without opening the cover; it cannot overcharge. The Ignitor is located on top of the gun, at the breech. It locks into firing position with a quarter-turn bayonet lock. To fire, pull the ignitor plunger up and then push down. These new improved parts are so accurate in their action that the gun can easily be loaded and fired in the dark. C. C. Hunter, Sales Manager, who will be in charge of the display at the Hotel McAlpin, also states that the Modle No. 66FG Conestoga Clear Vision Field Glass (not a toy) which has been very favorably received by the trade since it was recently placed on the market will also be shown. This Field Glass should prove of much interest to sporting goods buyers as well as toy buyers who purchase this type of product. The Conestoga Non-Skid Toy Track Silencers which are made of high quality elastic rubber and stop noise and prevents scratching of the floors or table will also be shown.

My first view of the G-Gun.

kind of hoax? A cruel trick left behind by Wily to torment me in my sleep?

What G-Gun? Was this a picture of it? My eyes raced over the text again and again, reading the rest of the page to be sure the illustration was indeed the G-Gun and not someone else's product. The only thing for sure is that it was new and it was called the G-Gun.

Distracted, I paged ahead through the volume. Later in this same April issue was a Conestoga ad showing the same illustration and underneath the words "Model 21GG BIG-BANG G-Gun". Collaborating testimony is sweet. Now, how to get one for my collection? But, along with the good news, there was bad news that day. In subsequent *Playthings* magazines after that issue there was no further mention of the G-Gun.

The hour-long train ride home offered a chance to reflect. What could this mean? Surely it must be die-cast like the pistol. If so, its survival rate would be much lower

The only G-Gun Ad...Ever.

than the cast iron cannons. Is this the rumored rifle that only reached prototype stage? They must have had a model or prototype to show at the Toy Fair. Please, please, at least a few dozen salesmen's samples. But did the buyers buy? Were orders so disappointing that production was canceled? Did they ever make the G-Gun at all?

I may never have a glass cannon. I can live with that. But, now the thought of another major Conestoga beyond my reach and may well be non-existent is... is untenable. A momentary wave of terror flashed through me.

Daily my hopes grew dimmer as one by one letters to cap gun and cannon collectors came back stating that, while they were familiar with Conestoga's pistol, they had never seen or heard of the G-Gun.

The story seemed closed with only these two items printed in *Playthings* as proof that there ever was a G-Gun. I was left wondering if they ever made the G-Gun at all.

Vincentine and I took a drive out to the Bethlehem-Allentown area early in March '92 to try and track down the old Conestoga factory buildings. From I-78 we took 378 north into Bethlehem.

We were watching for our exit to get to Conestoga Street when Vince saw a building to our right displaying the sign "Conestoga Court". Well, we could not get off 378 until Route 22, so we had no idea how to get back to that area.

It was time to pick up a county map and make use of the added detail therein. With map in hand, we eventually found Prospect St. and followed it in the direction of Conestoga St. only to be confronted with the great earthwork that supports the 378 highway.

After struggling with the inherent problems of one-way streets, we finally got across the highway further up and began picking our way back down to regain Prospect. Conestoga runs parallel to the river and 378 runs parallel also. When they put Route 378 in, they cut off forever the connection Conestoga St. had with Prospect St.

Now, here we were on Conestoga St. in Bethlehem, Pennsylvania looking at the only building there, Conestoga Court. The result of our journey is to arrive where we started and know it for the first time.

The building is now a condo and, we found out later, is neither the original factory nor Wily's office/residence. The site of those buildings is now under Route 378.

After a few photos we went and found 901-915 Cherokee St. where the Artillery Game was made and took pictures of that building as well. Time had flown, but we still had enough left to visit one antique store in Allentown and its proprietor Bob Lowe.

After struggling with small alleys and more one-way streets, Vince and I were rewarded with a most spacious display of early toys, magnificent stationary steam engines and firearms. A real treat compared to the crowded

901-915 Cherokee Street, So. Bethlehem, P.A.

aisles at the best toy shows.

About half way around the store, there was a 6F box that was inside a show case and I made a mental note to ask for a better look before we left. Then my eyes drifted about the rest of the case and then to the top of it where there was a Wright Flyer on top of a box. On top of the case were stored several long boxes wrapped in newsprint, but the one under the Flyer was different.

On the end panel was a picture of the G-GUN and the words "1-BIG-BANG AUTOMATIC G-GUN". Oh! Heart be still!

Was this a dream? Could my eyes be trusted? I tried

to call Vince who was not ten feet away, but my voice would not work. Then she saw me and knew from my expression that this was verrrry serious.

That box would not have lasted all these years unless there was a G-Gun inside it. My heart raced with anticipation of seeing, for the first time, the 21GG which I had already dismissed as non existent.

Bob opened the box. The colors, two tone, dark olive drab and deep maroon were at once in conflict and then

Oh! Heart....

just as quickly very much at home together on this magnificent pre-war toy. I touched the cool metal and then lifted it out. But wait! It's not die-cast at all. This G-Gun is iron and steel and brass. Well I'll be.... It was at this moment I knew I must have it! How does it work? My mind lusted for the details.

Being familiar with both carbide guns and firearms, I had no trouble deciphering the design. The bolt has at its rear top a small metal tab that begs me to press it down and when I do it allows the bolt to move back about 5/8" exposing a 3/8" x 1" slot on the left side of the breech. This opening is where I will vent the chamber in between shots. A brass pin keeps the bolt from moving any farther back, but when I lift it the bolt is easily removed completely.

With the bolt out, I can see the ports for admitting fresh air and where the spark is produced. The flint tube and the adjusting screw are clearly visible just forward of the trigger.

The charging plunger is commuted completely through the length of the bolt and at the very front is where the charge is metered out. The large set screw near the front of the bolt is the cover for the Bangsite magazine.

I put the bolt back in and it clicks home with that satisfying combination of metallic gun noises like a real firearm. A plunger protrudes from the bolt's rear and when the bolt locks in place, I find my thumb following the plunger down. I imagine the hiss of the carbide and water making acetylene. The trigger needs no instruction and I squeeze it slowly cocking the spring that releases suddenly with a snap, sending a shower of sparks to their appointed duty.

I must become the custodian for this rare engineering tour-de-force. This may be the only G-Gun in the universe. I know if I don't buy it now, there will be no next time. The 21-GG followed us home.

That night as I fell asleep I thought to myself, "What could be the only surviving G-Gun in the world is now in my possession. A fitting reward for my research. No longer shall I envy the Caribbean treasure hunters who, after years of research in Spain, found wrecked galleons loaded with gold on the sea floor. I have my own treasure, the G-Gun." Just as I nodded off, I reached under my pillow and touched it one more time.

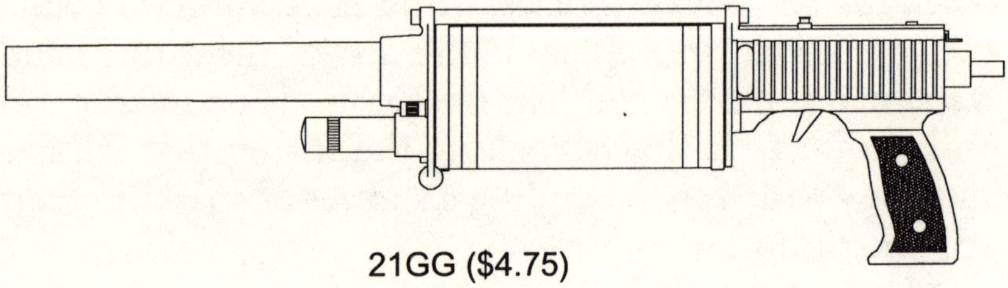

21GG ($4.75)

The G-Gun.

CHAPTER TEN

OTHER CARBIDE CANNONS

While it could be said that the BIG-BANG is the only carbide cannon, and very few could dispute it, this in fact would not be true. Viewing Wily's success with envy, other manufactures wanted in and there are no less than fifteen patents granted for toy gas cannons between 1924 and 1937. Of the fifteen, only four are found in the advertising record and only two have survived in numbers to this day. Surprisingly, several of the patents are assigned to the Kilgore Manufacturing Company, famous for their cap guns, but they never produced any carbide cannons.

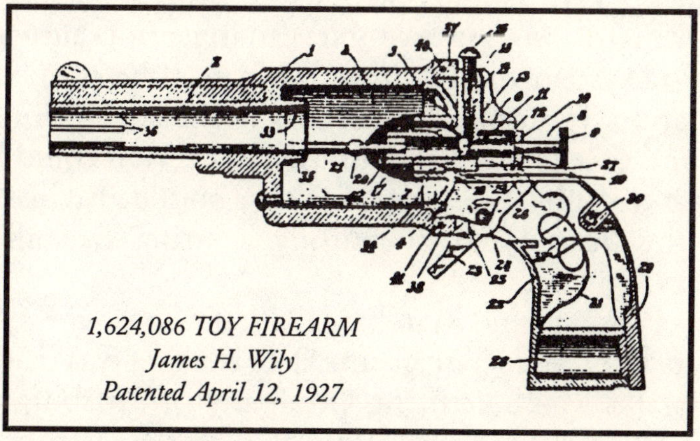

The Major Graphic From Wily's Pistol Patent.

64 PLAYTHINGS December, 1928

"TOYS THAT MAKE A NOISE"
NEW
4th OF JULY ITEMS
"SAF-TY CANNON"

A modern looking gas cannon making a very loud noise, fired by paper caps. An absolutely new idea. Fired by pulling a string like all real artillery.

Length, 20 inches
Height, 7 inches
Weight, 10 lbs.

No. 210 Howitzer—"Saf-ty Cannon" $4.00 each east of Rockies. All features of this new cannon covered by patents pending.

At Ten Pounds the No. 210 Howitzer was a serious challenge to the 16F.

Advertised one time only, in December 1928, by the Dayton Toy & Specialty Company, the makers of *Son-ny* toys, is the No. 210 Howitzer. This toy is based on patent #1,765,562 assigned to C. C. Blackmore of Dayton, Ohio.

It is a very detailed piece using either flint, a cap or both for ignition. It incorporates an ingenious automatic charging system that requires the breech be opened for ventilation. From the dimensions in the ad, 20" long, 7" high and a weight of ten pounds, this cannon could hold its own with the 16F. The ad takes a shot at BIG-BANG with the line "Fired by pulling a string like all *real* artillery".

In February and March of 1930, the Krasher Kannon appears in *Playthings* magazine. The Krasher was made by the Forster Manufacturing Company of Pittsburgh Pa. and is based on the invention of Birger Engstrom outlined in patent #1,807,974, assigned to the Forster Manufacturing Company. This toy used an internal rotating set

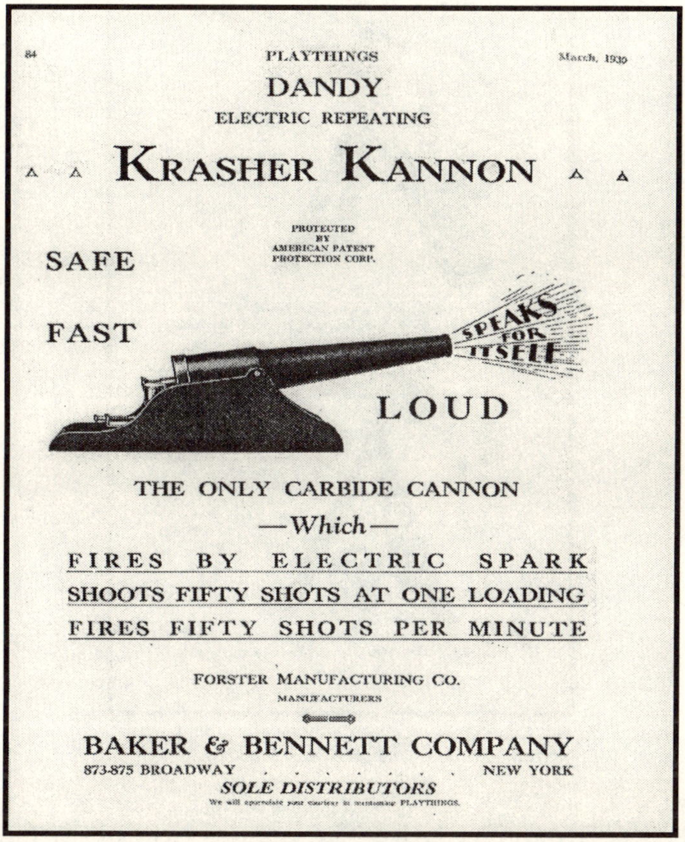

Krasher Ad, Playthings, March 1930.

of three firing chambers. While one was fired, one was open to the atmosphere where fresh air was scavenged in, and the third was closed to all but the gas source where the explosive charge was formed.

The two survivors were both manufactured by Smith's Welding Equipment Corporation of Minneapolis Minnesota. They are the Model 31, Automatic Machine Gun, better know as the Big Shot, and the Model 32, Rapid Fire Machine Gun. The Big Shot and the Rapid Fire were both marketed by Wily and they appear side-by-side in a 1933 Conestoga advertisement.

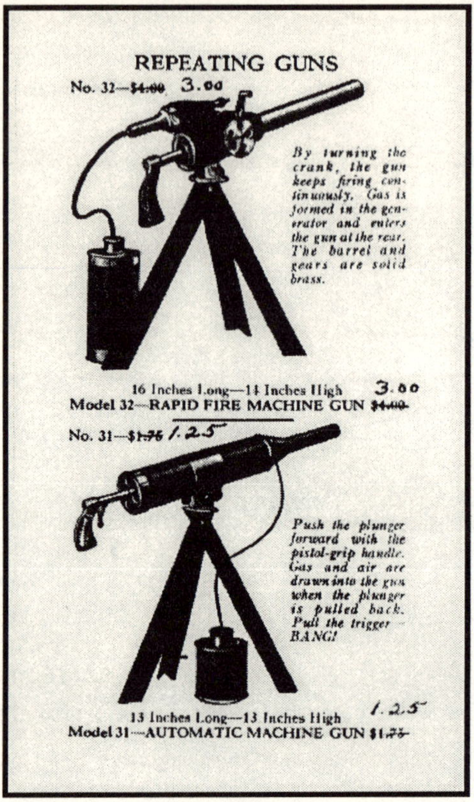

Both Smith's guns were marketed by Wily.

Unfortunately, complete reproduction of the patents is outside the scope of this book, but copies of patents may be obtained from the U.S. Patent Office (see below). However, since I have piqued your interest, here are the major drawings with patent numbers of all the carbide patents uncovered in my search.

Printed copies of any patent, identified by its patent number, may be purchased from the Patent and Trademark Office at a cost of $1.50 each, postage free.

Patent and Trademark Office (703) 537-7800
Department of commerce
Washington, DC 20231

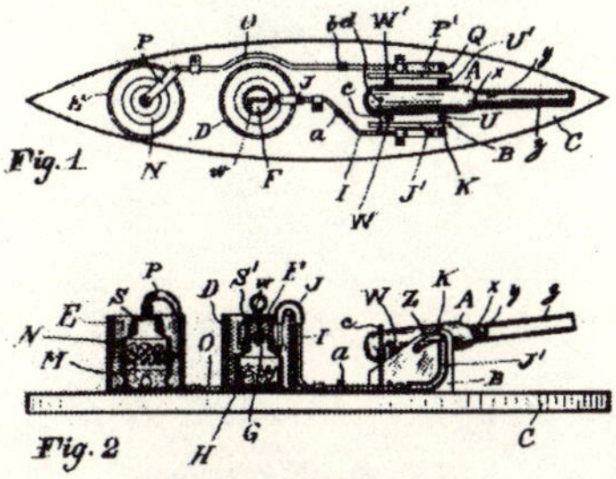

1,057,420. GAS GUN.
Nelson Goodyear
Patented April 1, 1913

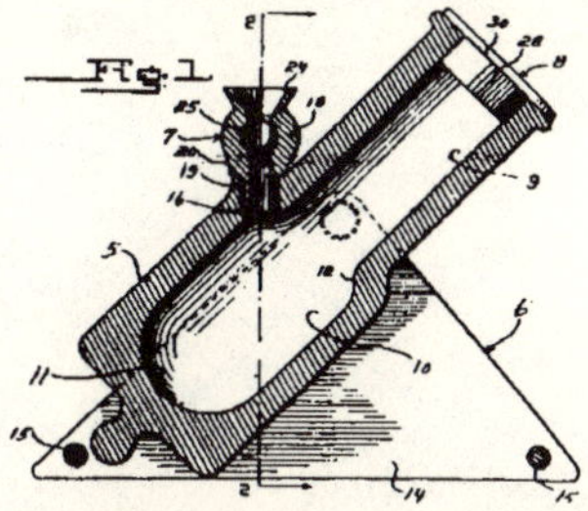

1,757,523 TOY GAS CANNON
Max F. Grimm
Patented May 6, 1930

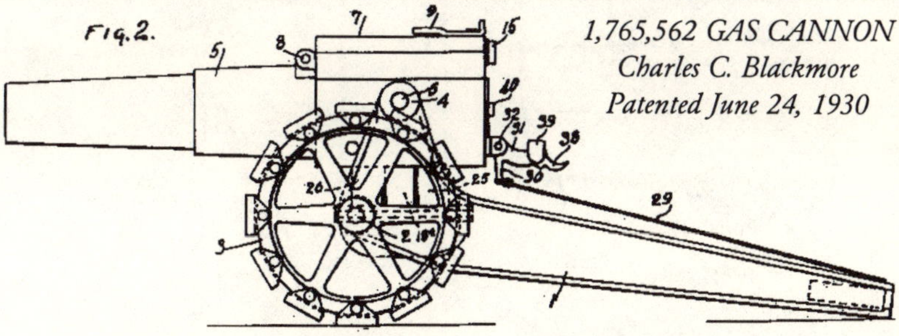

1,765,562 GAS CANNON
Charles C. Blackmore
Patented June 24, 1930

Dayton Toy & Specialty Company's #210 Howitzer

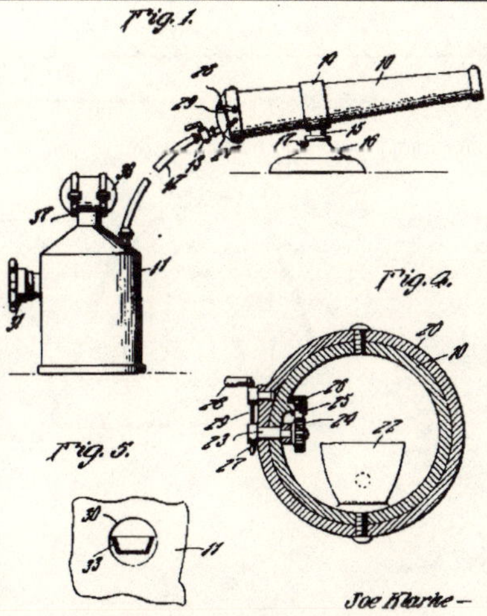

1,597,447 GAS CANNON
Joe Klarke
Patented August 24, 1926

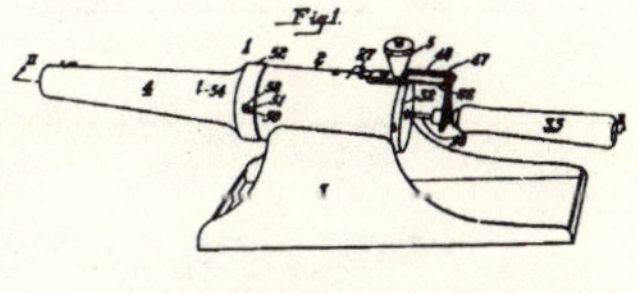

1,789,585 GAS CANNON
Samuel Gormly
Patented January 20, 1931

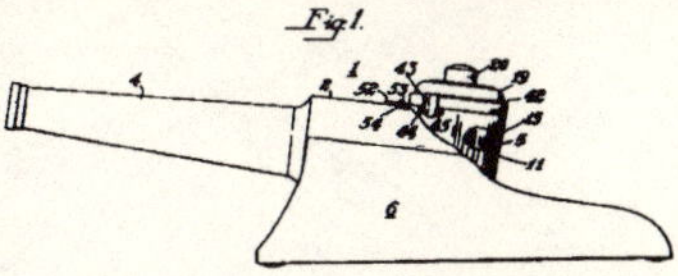

1,806,633 TOY GAS CANNON
John W. MacDonald
Patented May 26, 1931

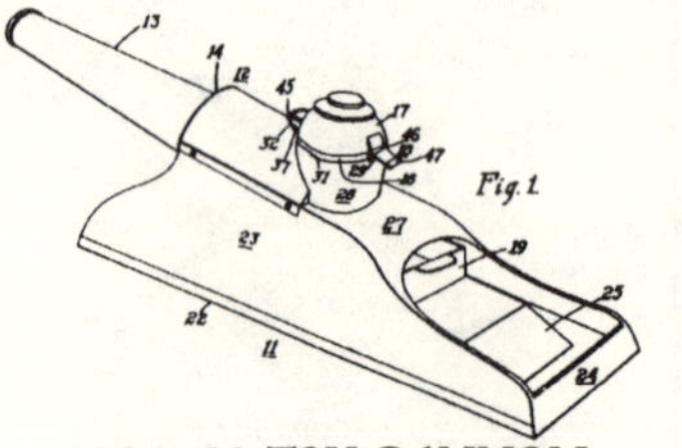

1,806,693 TOY CANNON
John W. MacDonald
Patented May 26, 1931

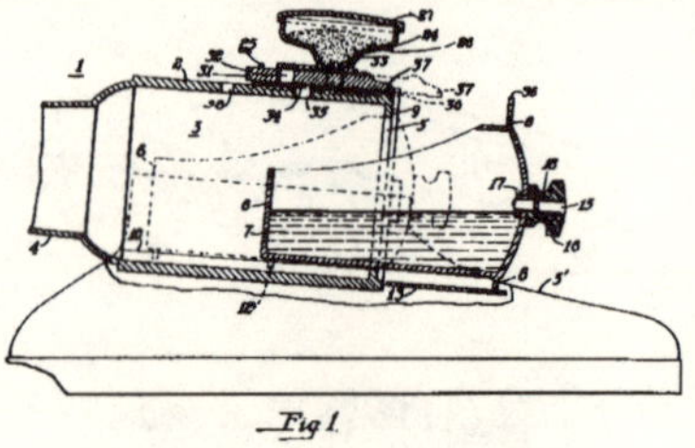

1,863,062 TOY CANNON
John W. MacDonald
Patented June 14, 1932

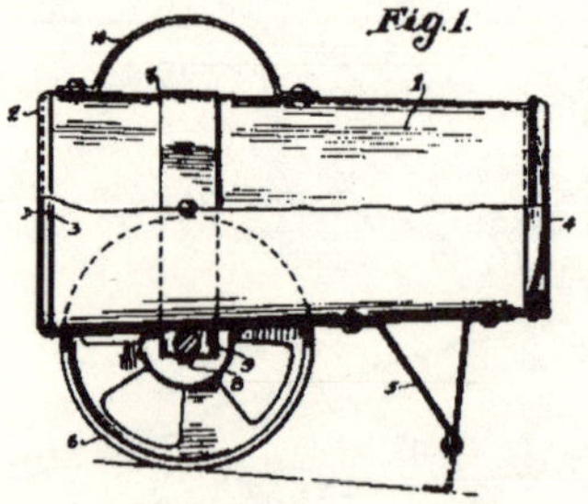

1,854,679 TOY CANNON
George W. Walker & Tomas Peek
Patented April 19, 1932

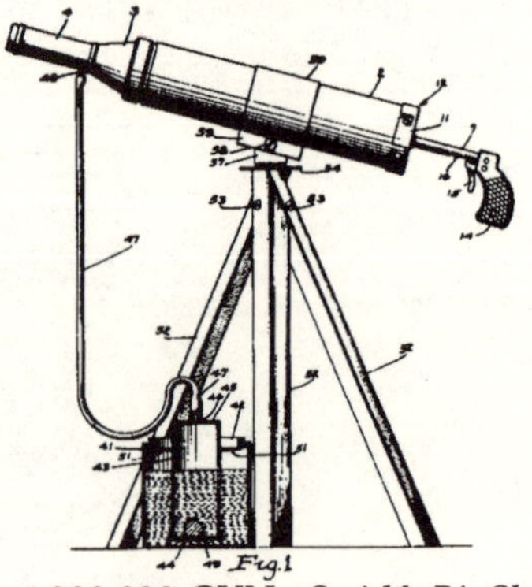

1,883,028 GUN Smith's Big-Shot
Elmer H. Smith
Patented October 18, 1932

1,807,974 TOY CANNON
Birger Engstrom
Patented June 2, 1931

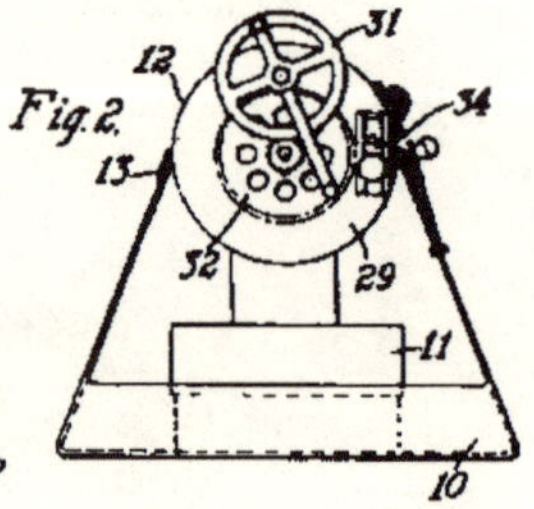

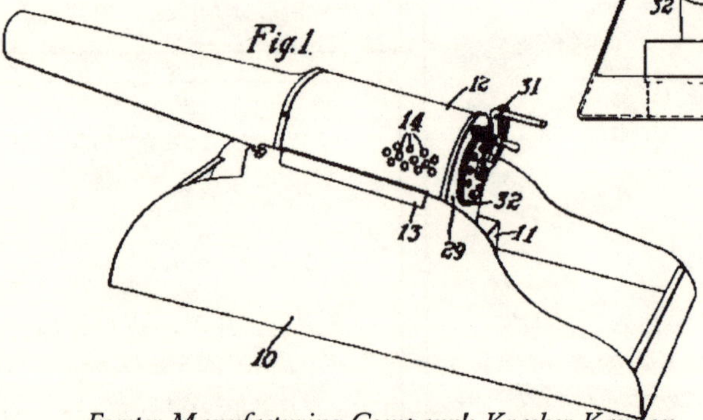

Forster Manufacturing Company's Krasher Kannon.

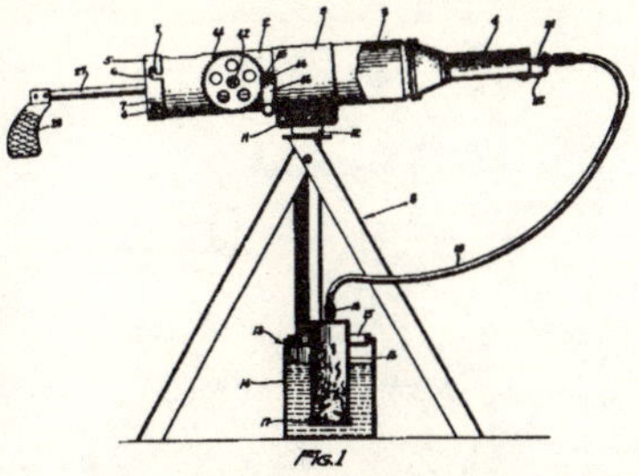

1,883,029 MACHINE GUN
Elmer H. Smith
Patented October 18, 1932

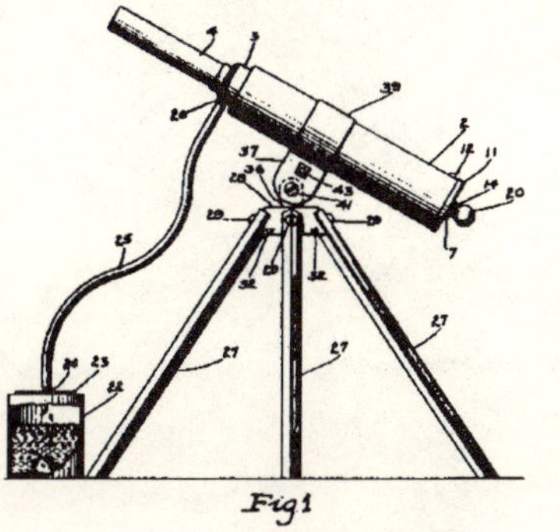

1,908,070 GUN
Elmer H. Smith
Patented May 9, 1933

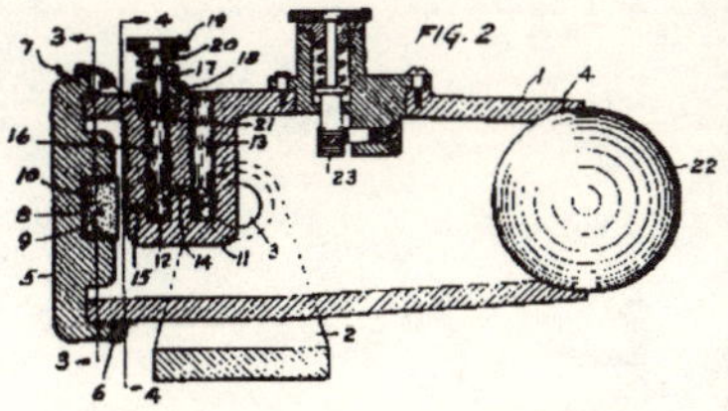

1,999,357 CANNON
Louis L. Driggs, Jr. (Kilgore)
Patented April 30, 1935

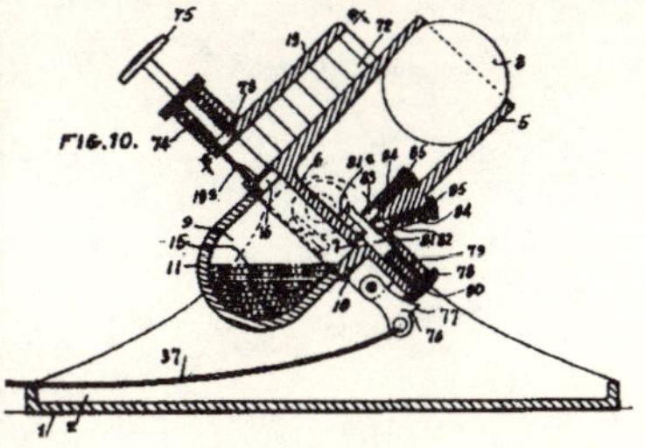

2,000,607 GAS CANNON
Edward S. Peake
Patented May 7, 1935

1,998,023 GAS CANNON
Edward S. Peake (Kilgore)
Patented April 16, 1935

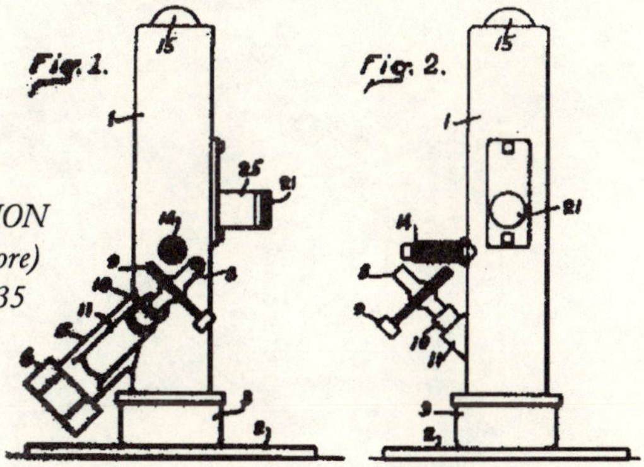

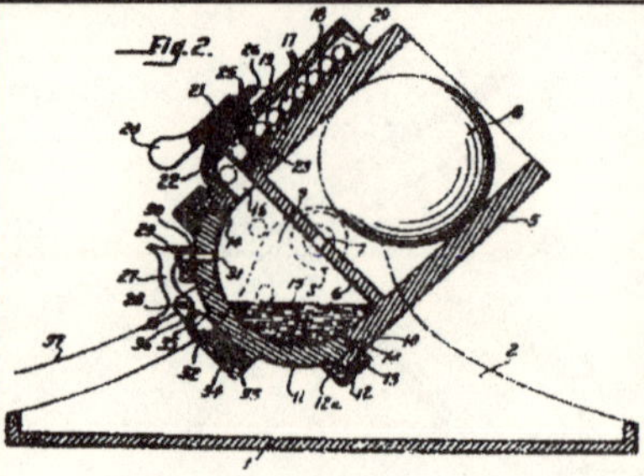

1,970,017 GAS CANNON
Edwars S. Peake (Kilgore)
Patented August 14, 1934

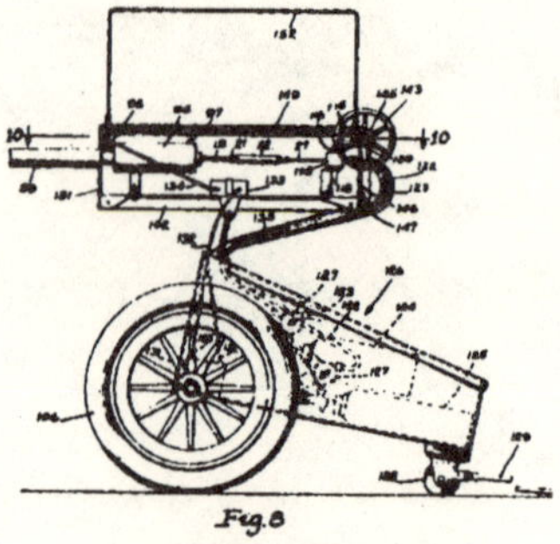

2,094,854 GUN
Elmer H. Smith
Patented October 5, 1937

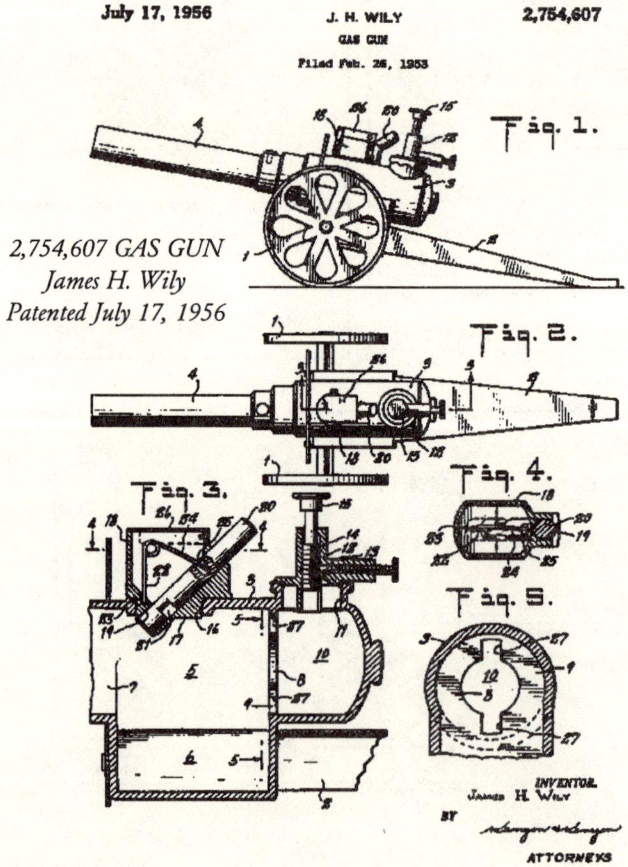

2,754,607 GAS GUN
James H. Wily
Patented July 17, 1956

CHAPTER ELEVEN

REPAIR & RESTORATION

When you find a broken cannon, chances are good that there will be several parts that are OK. I try to buy these damaged toys if only for the few good parts there are, providing the price is right. If there are pieces missing, ask about them. Sometimes the dealer will have them and just has not set them out. Broken cast iron can be silver soldered or brazed together and if you have all the bits, find a good welder and go for it. With skill and luck the resulting repair can be invisible.

Todays broken toy is tomorrow's spare parts.

Cleaning

Normal dust and dirt from the years may be removed with warm soapy water. Try not to polish the brass parts, the patina takes years to form and polished parts will look like they were replaced. Never use a wire brush, an old tooth brush works well.

The biggest problem with carbide guns is calcium build-up where the gas is generated. Calcium is a by-product of the acetylene producing process and if left in the cannon, it will harden almost like cement. You can prevent this accumulation by thoroughly rinsing out the barrel immediately after use.

The calcium can be loosened by chipping through the breech or charger opening with a screw driver. A bent wire is useful for getting around corners. Mechanically remove as much as you can in this way before using chemicals.

I have found muriatic acid (available from hardware supply for cleaning masonry) very useful for softening and removing the calcium. Muriatic acid is a 20% solution of hydrochloric acid. Be sure to use latex gloves and safety glasses. Be careful, read the label.

Hydrochloric acid attacks iron oxide (rust), so any rust spots on your cannon exposed to the acid will come out bright. This may not be desirable as it can make a cannon look like it was repainted and made to look old by distressing the paint. The acid also attacks iron and pot metal, but at a much slower rate so that should not be a concern. The acid will also discolor paint so avoid using it on the exterior of your cannons. Never leave anything in acid overnight.

Repainting

I will never repaint a cannon unless it was already repainted or if a repair such as welding warrants it. Some times there will be so little original paint left that a toy should be repainted. If you must repaint, use only the original colors. For the old guns, that would be black for all but the wheels, which are red. The newer cannons are a green-gold color that is not commercially available. I had to have the color specially mixed. This step is expensive, but I recommend it when you are not painting the whole piece but only touching up a replaced part or a repair. I bought a Bombing Plane that was missing the tail. This part was not too difficult to replicate, so I did. I had paint mixed to match the wing and except for my initials and the date vibro-engraved in the bottom of the tail, no one would know it was not the original.

Axles

In the older field pieces, the most common damage is broken axles. The axle is an integral part of the drag casting and usually breaks off cleanly. I have a method to fix this and the repair is quite sturdy and is impossible to detect without disassembling the piece. The axle drawing (p. 148) is the replacement axle which can be made in any machine shop using a lathe. The drag is drilled and reamed on center to 0.3125 diameter and the new axle is pressed in from the inside out. Replace the wheel and cinch ring and re-assemble the cannon.

Conestoga's replacement cinch rings are actually sheet metal speed nuts and are OK for holding wheels on, but are unsatisfactory for restoration. Make your own authentic cinch rings from 1/16" diameter copper plated iron welding wire. Coil the wire tightly around a 1/4" diameter dowel then snip rings from this coil as you need them with a wire cutter.

The length of the replacement axle is determined by the thickness of the wheel hub and the thickness of the part of the drag where the axle is pressed through. Add these two dimensions and then add an additional 1/32" (0.03125) for clearance and this should be your dimension from the flange to the ring groove.

If the drag already has a hole in it from a previous repair (this is common) or your fit is not quite the press it should have been, use silicone seal between the flange and the drag. This provides an excellent bond with resilience in this high stress area. Silicone drives paint crazy, so don't smear it all about.

Breech Blocks/Ignition

Roughly one out of three old cannons will still have its breech block. Consider yourself lucky if any old breech block you come across is still serviceable.

The worst breech block by far was one I got with a 10W. The metal was all cracked and flaky. I am told this is the result of contaminated metal used in the casting or years of temperature extremes from being stored in unheated space.

Broken breech blocks are difficult to repair even if you have all the pieces. Epoxy or super glue the bits together. It will be nice for show, but will probably fail at the repair if it is used.

The most common thing missing from intact blocks is the charging measure. These measures were made of tin plated steel of a very thin gauge and in the often damp confines of the combustion chamber, they just rusted away. You can get replacements from Conestoga or fashion your own from a bit of brass hobby tubing, old TV antenna or tin can. The easiest one to make yourself is just a bit of brass welding wire 1/32" diameter with a .22

caliber rifle shell soldered to the end. Use a .22 short for the 7F, 8F and 11F and use a .22 long for the 12F and 16F. Electrical tape the shank to the breech block so that the shell is pointed down when the block is locked to the cannon.

One common problem with breech blocks is frozen mechanisms and corroded flints. Soak the block in kerosene or any other light oil for a few days then gently, oh! so gently, try to work the parts loose.

I start by trying to unscrew the flint adjusting screw (all threads are right hand and loosen by turning counter-clockwise). Removing this first gets it out of the way (if you snap the head off you are in real trouble), the spring and flint might just fall out (if you are lucky) and a new channel is opened for penetrating oil to reach the plunger.

Using two pliers, one to hold the plunger shaft and one to hold the knob, I remove the knob from the end of the plunger. Once this knob is off, I clear forward of the plunger with a drill by hand, then try to tap the plunger out. If the plunger moves a little but is reluctant to go further, tap it back and forth, giving it a little soak in between until you finally work it out.

Now both ends of the flint hole are accessible and jammed flint may be drilled out or driven down into the plunger hole where it will fall free or may be snapped off. Refer to the breech block cut-away drawings (p. 92) when determining what size drill bits to use for clearing holes.

Chargers

The biggest problem with chargers is the plunger gets jammed in the down position and then some one tries to unscrew the charger from the cannon. The extended plunger scrapes against the inside of the cannon and keeps the charger from unscrewing and the plunger gets nicked making it even harder to retract.

Remove the barrel if possible. With the charger screwed all the way in put a sturdy screw driver down the barrel hole and try to force the plunger up to the retracted position. Once the plunger is up there should be no problem unscrewing the charger from the gun.

Professional Repair

If the scope of your particular restoration project is beyond your skills, you may wish to consult a professional. As interest and value in antique toys grow, more and more craftsmen are advertising in the antique journals. One whose talents and capacity lends itself to the repair of BIG-BANGS is Russ Harrington. You can reach Russ at :

Russ Harrington (401) 687-8596
1805 Wilson Point Rd.
Baltimore, MD 21220

CHAPTER TWELVE

HOME MADE CANNONS

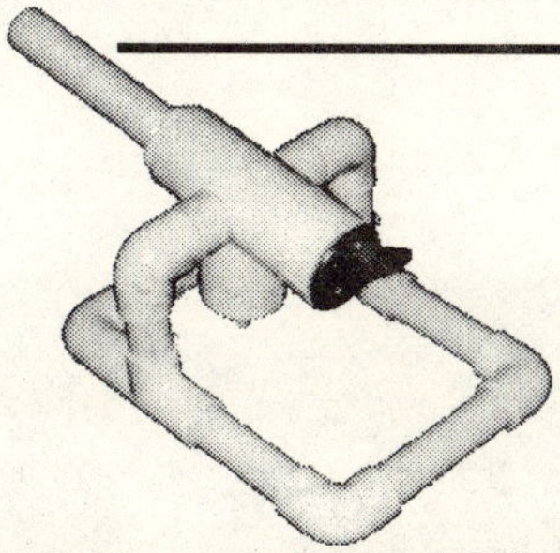

During one of my visits with David Spinosa, he mentioned that plans for a plastic carbide cannon had appeared in *Popular Mechanics* magazine around July 1976 for the Bi-Centennial. A search through *Popular Mechanics* of that year and also *Popular Science* turned up nothing. I then wrote to these magazines asking about the cannon. No luck.

All this time, the idea of a plastic cannon made more and more sense to me. PVC pipe fittings are available in a wide range of sizes and shapes. They are used in many applications other than plumbing. Failing to find the magazine plans, I decided to design my own plastic cannon.

Driving to work I fantasized about a carbide cannon made from 4" pipe, that would wake 'em up! Finally, after several trips to the local plumbing supply and eyeing the available fittings, the plans were laid down for the barrel. I had not yet arrived at a design for the carriage that I was comfortable with.

The body was just a tee with a threaded socket in the bull and in one run. The other run had a reducing bushing into which the barrel was cemented. The bull, when plugged, would be the water sump. Now for the breech.

One of the things I always marveled at was the breeches on the big guns. The breech plug was a big screw with half the threads cut away. In the breech was a matching socket of the opposite sex. The plug would swing in and with only a quarter turn would engage and lock all those rows of giant threads! A mute testimony to the power of the gun, the breech having to withstand the firing forces.

My PVC cannon would have a real breech block.

I was determined to have such a breech on my PVC cannon. After much carving (by hand), the PVC parts were ready. A charging spoon was attached and the banana clips mounted for a remote piezo-ignition system. The breech action did not work as well as I had hoped, but proper shimming of the breech gasket resulted in a good tight seal with about one eighth of a turn. My cannon collector friend David Ross was coming to visit, so in spite of the temptation to shoot the thing, I waited for Dave.

President's day, 1992. Dave and his lovely daughter Melissa came to visit. Vincentine and Melissa went to the mall and Dave and I went to the garage. The cannon was still without a carriage, so it had to be hand held. Dave held it while I pushed the button. BLAM-0! I was pleased with the results. Next I held it and Dave touched it off.

Again a healthy report (and a little kick too!). For the next shot I suggested we patch a wine cork down the barrel and see if we could dent an aluminum can. Well, I don't know what happened. I missed the can that was only about two feet away but I didn't miss the window pane in the door. Bang - Crash - Tinkle. Dave looked at the window, and then at me and then laughed (he didn't have to fix the window).

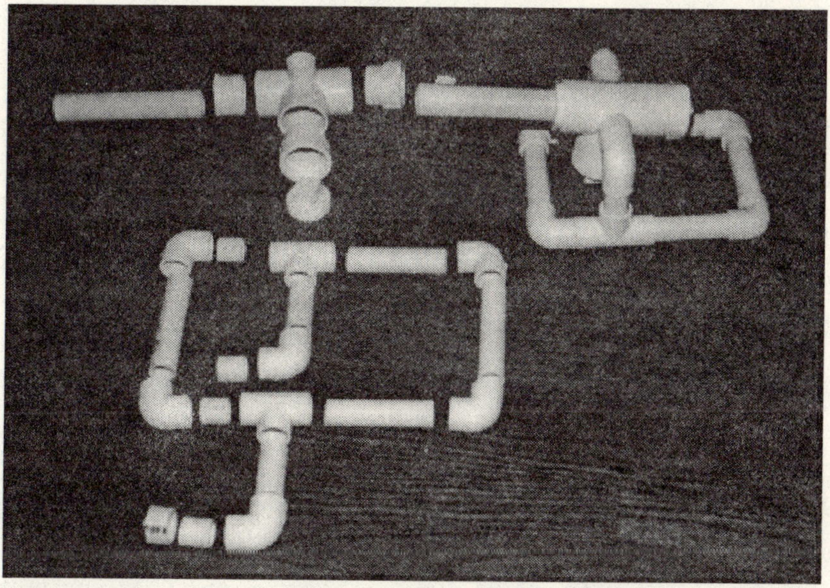

Parts laid out on left, assembled cannon on right.

I abandoned the big-gun-breech in favor of just screwing in the plug. It takes about three turns to get it closed and this produces a built in time delay, allowing the gas to form. This final version of the cannon I've named the MkII-B.

You can make this cannon for about ten dollars with touch hole ignition; a bit more if you use a gas grill piezo device. It will help if you can get to a lathe to turn down

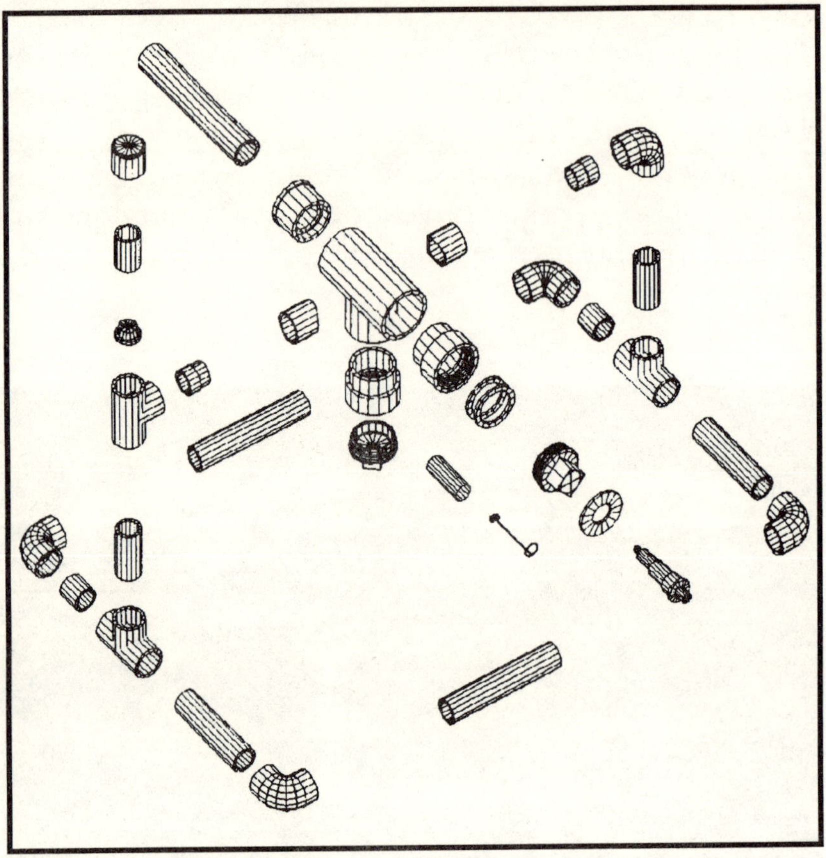

PVC MK-IIB, "Exploded" View.

the bearings and access to metric taps for the piezo gadget is a big plus.

The original plastic cannon? Oh, yeah, I finally checked with *Mechanix Illustrated* and bingo! June 1976, page 38. A two page article by Hal Kelly has plans for a huge carbide cannon using three and four inch PVC pipe. I can't wait to build one. I'll bet from here in New Jersey, I can break Dave's garage windows up there in Connecticut.

APPENDIX

The appendix is provided as a further reference of BIG-BANG celebrators. Most toys are drawn in plan and elevation views. Although there are no BIG-BANG reproductions as of this printing, dimensions are provided against the day they may be needed. It will be noted that even among authentic pieces, there is some variation in barrel lengths due to casting methods. In the photographs, Alex, a Marx soldier, is employed to provide vertical scale. Alex is 3 7/16" tall. For horizontal scale, a Bangsite tube, 5 5/8" long is used.

Wily used a simple, no-nonsense, nomenclature when giving model numbers to his celebrators. It is simple to the point of abstraction, so I will explain it. The numerical part of the model number refers to the barrel length and the letter or letters following are the toy's initials. For example; model 7F had a 7 inch barrel and was a Field piece. Here are the letters used and what they stand for: F = Field piece, FR = Field piece noise Regulation, D = Defense, W = Wheel, P = Pistol or Plane, B = Boat, FC = Field piece/Charger, T = Tank (I use 5TA for the Army tank and 5TM for the Motor tank), GG = G-Gun, MM = Millimeter.

Each toy's description begins with the model number followed by the years the toy was in production. This in turn is followed by the author's comments. Finally any markings are listed and any notes about the breech block, magazine etc. and the toy's weight. Weights were measured with breech block in place with no water or Bangsite present.

The New Prices are a list of years and the toy's corresponding prices. Prices are shown for only those years that can be documented. These prices are especially useful for dating cannons that have survived with their papers or box. If you have a 6F in the box and the price on the box is $3.95, then you will find your cannon was made in the late 1950's.

My price guide is only a guide. It is difficult to come up with numbers from so narrow a sample. I have endeavored to provide prices for three levels of condition. These prices are what I would expect to buy the cannons for. *In Box* is just that. The high end would be mint or near mint and the low end would be satisfied with an intact box and a complete toy. *Good* is a complete toy with no missing or broken parts. The high side would have very nice paint with little or no rust. *Poor* condition are those cannons that are missing breech blocks, chargers or other parts or have broken parts or are heavily rusted. The more parts missing or broken, the less it is worth. Sometimes these are a good buy just for parts.

Here is a pricing example; a complete 7F with breech block in sound condition is worth $125. Without the breech block, it is only worth $75 because you can get a new breech block from Conestoga for about $50. Break an axle and it is only worth $60. Missing or broken wheels are only a problem with the 16F and the 10W with tear drop wheels. All other wheels are available from Conestoga.

Establishing rareness is another problem facing the author. I was surprised to have gotten almost every BIG-BANG in the relatively short period of four years. During that time, I kept a list of every carbide cannon I saw and to that list I have added cannons known in other collections. From all this I can only say that some models are very hard to find, some are very easy to find and the rest are out there and will take some time to find. I have employed a degree system similar to that used in the book Cast Iron Toy Guns and Capshooters. Authors Sam Logan and Charles Best used six degrees represented by zero to five stars (*), but I prefer bombs.

One bomb (💣) means it is easy to find. Two bombs (💣💣) means you can find it, but it may take a while. Three bombs (💣💣💣) means it is scarce and if you find one, you are lucky.

All you have to do to find these old cannons is to start looking. Poke through every antique shop you find. Antique toy shows are always fun. Subscribe to any or all of the periodicals listed in the appendix for a schedule of antique shows and auctions. Some of the newer cannons will turn up at yard sales, but I have had my best results at the antique flea markets and swapping with other collectors.

Every effort has been made to make the information in this book as accurate and informative as possible. I encourage you to correspond with me by writing to:

Raymond V. Brandes
RAY-VIN PUBLISHING CO.
P.O. BOX 11435-E
NEW BRUNSWICK, NJ 08906

Chargers

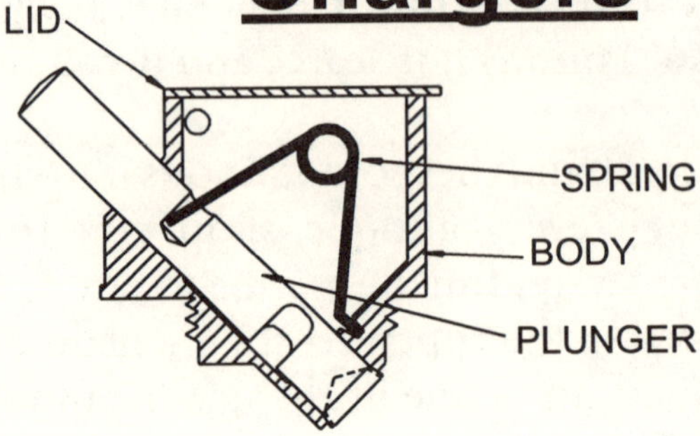

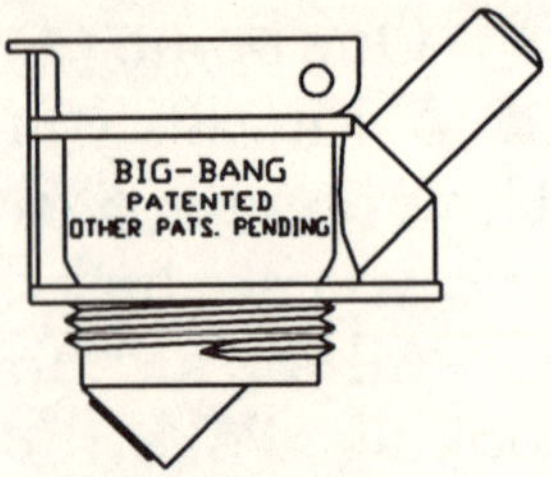

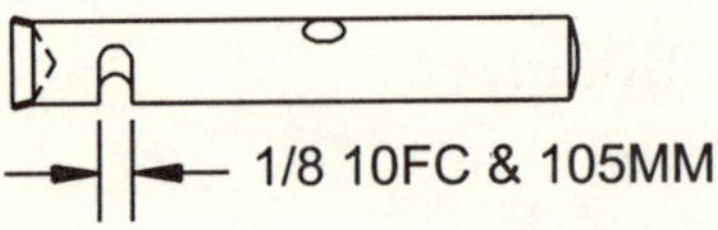

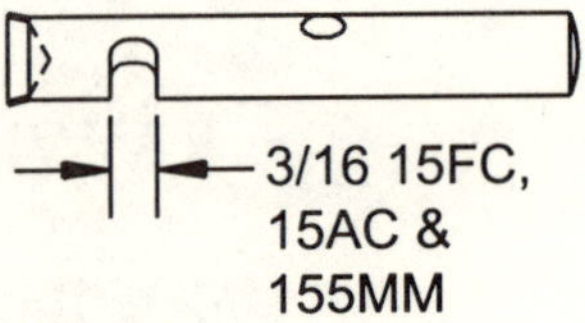

In spite of what is marked on the charger lid you may experience poor performance if the wrong plunger is fitted to your cannon. Check the dimensions of the Bangsite slot in your charger.

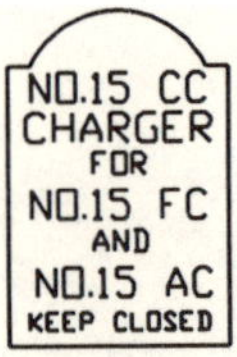

Original charger lid from 15AC.
This is the earliest example.

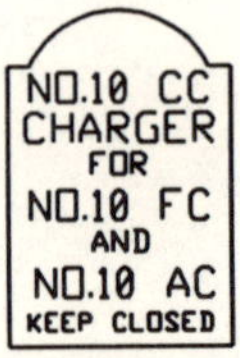

Orginal charger lid from 10FC.
The 10AC was never made.

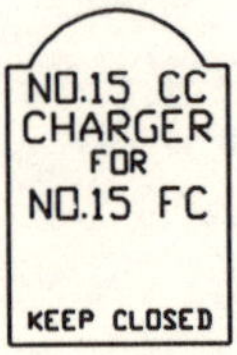

15AC was removed from the lid
when the model was dropped.

Lid of replacement charger purchased
by author, November 1991.

AVERAGE CARBIDE CHARGES FOR VARIUS CHARGING SYSTEMS

Chargers: B = Breech block, C = Charger, S = Spoon

5T	6F	10FC	15FC	2"	3"	4"	G-GUN
B	B	C	C	S	S	S	C
100 charges - weigh in grains:							
40	55	103	174	167	306	462	247
Average charge - weight in grains:							
0.4	0.55	1.03	1.74	1.67	3.06	4.62	2.47
Average charge - weight in miligrams:							
26	36	67	113	108	198	299	160

The 5T breech block is used only on the 5T Army Tank.

The 6F breech block is used on the 6F and the Bombing Plane.

The 10FC is used on the 10FC and the 105MM.

The 15FC is used on the 15FC, 15AC and the 155MM.

The 2" spoon is used in the 7D, 7F, 8F, 8FR and the Gunboat.

The 3" spoon is used in the 11D, 11F, 12F and the 12FR.

The 4" spoon is used in the 16F.

The G-Gun charger is used in the G-Gun.

BREECH BLOCKS

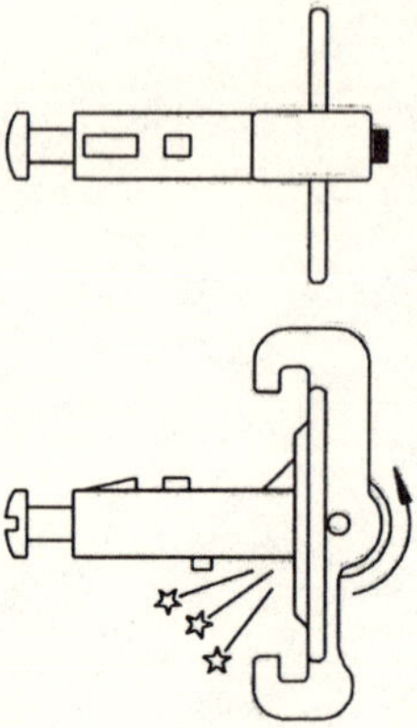

Wheel Type

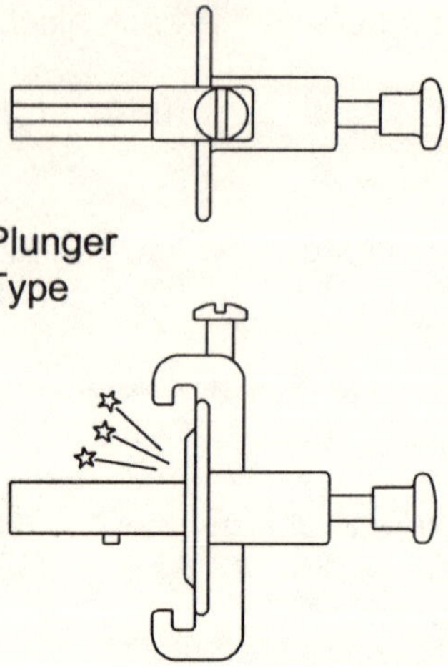

Plunger Type

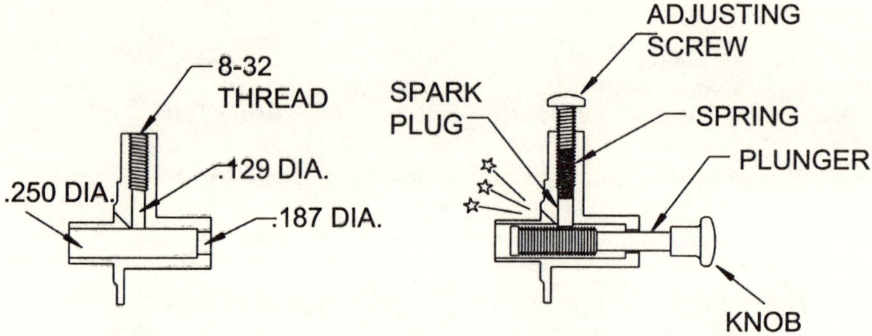

5T-ARMY TANK

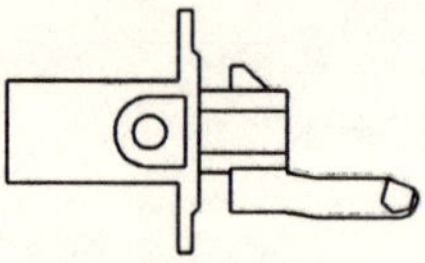

ALL OTHER

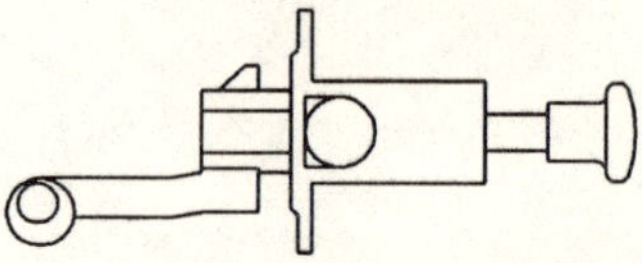

BAYONET TYPE

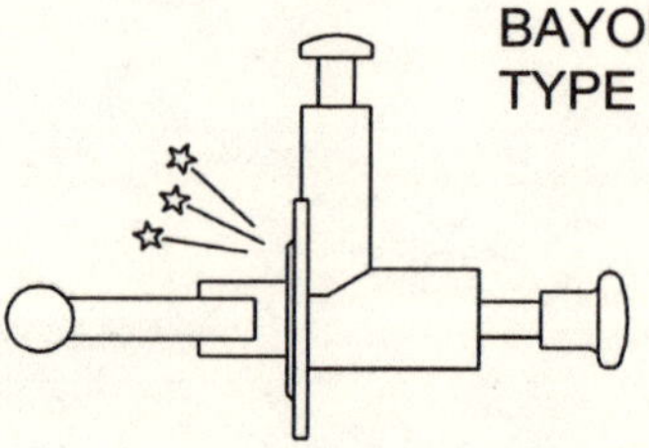

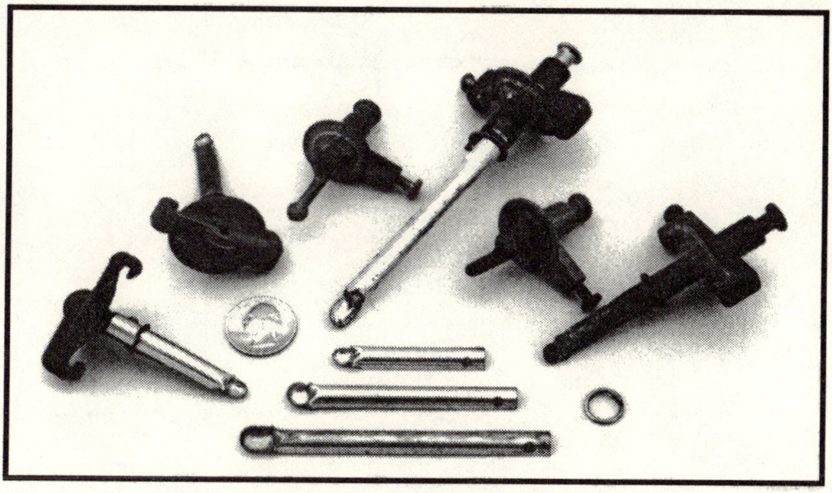

Breech Blocks. (Left to Right) Two Wheel types with 2" spoons, standard bayonet type, Replacement lug type with 4" spoon, 5T Army Tank bayonet, Original lug type with 3" spoon. Foreground 2" spoon, 3" spoon, 4" spoon and spoon clamp ring. The charger model breech blocks (not pictured) are the standard bayonet type with the Bangsite measure sniped off.

THE ARTILLERY GAME

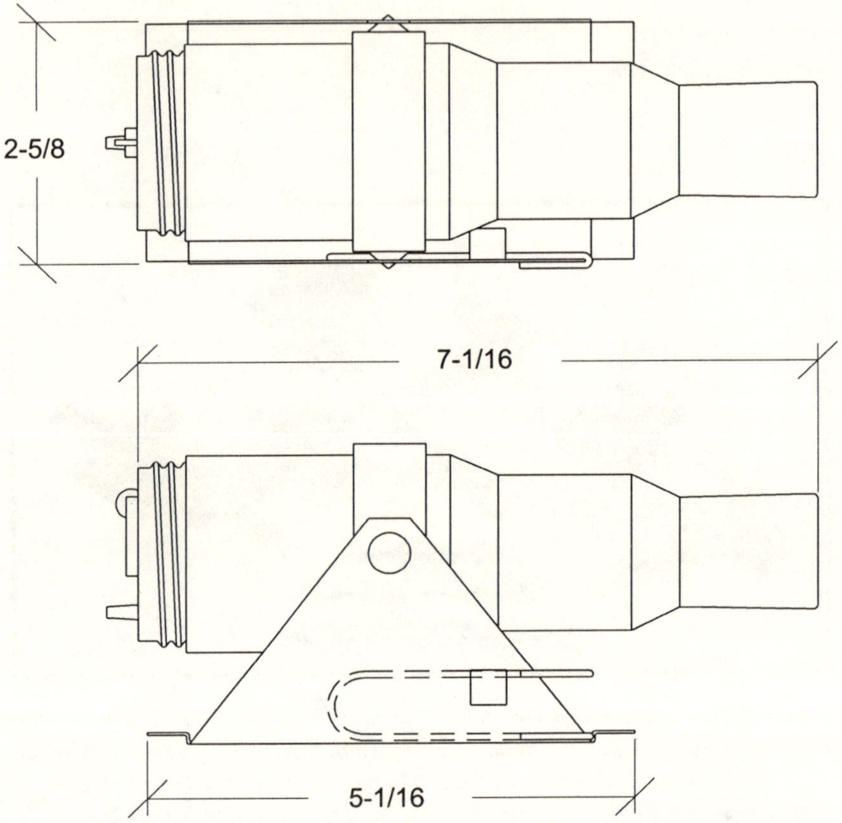

THE ARTILLERY GAME, 1915

The Artillery Game is the first carbide cannon we find nationally advertised. Only made for one year and because of the glass barrel this model is difficult to find. It is said only 5000 were produced.

I suspect the Artillery Game used the same gas generator as did the Gas Cannon but it benefited from the newly developed flint ignition. Apparently there were several revisions in the design because the end panel on the wooden Artillery Game box at Conestoga shows it to be a model "E".

Also on the end of the box is "PATENTED 1907 - OTHER PATENTS APPLIED FOR". Franklin's Patent was granted in 1907.

Price Guide Artillery Game
Poor - $75 - $150
Good - $150 - $300
In Box - $300 - $600
New Prices: 1915 - $1.00

THE GAS CANNON

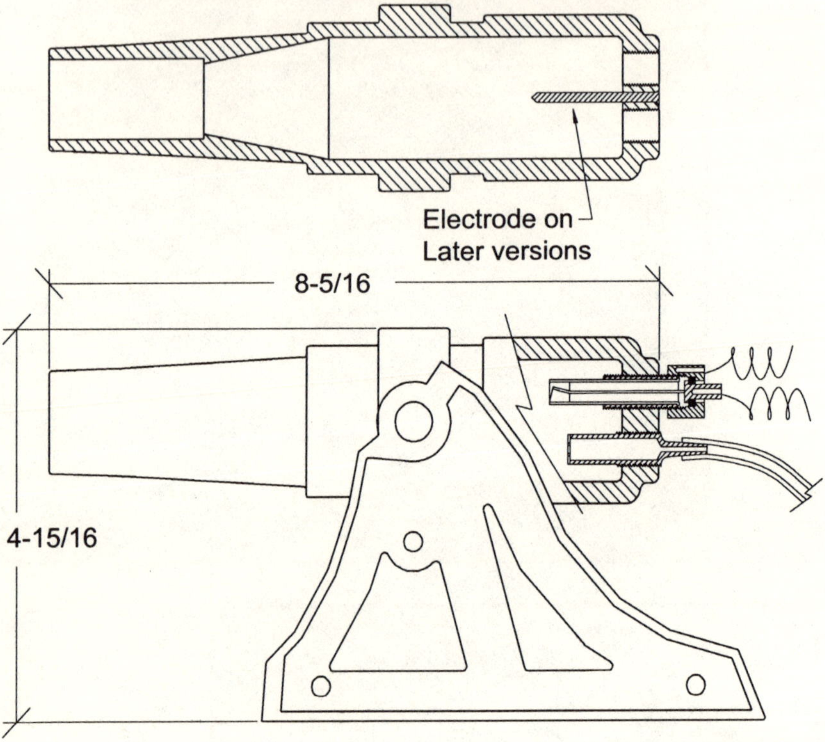

The Gas Cannon, 1912 - 1914

This appears to be the first commercial carbide cannon. The barrel is cast iron and is supported by two cast iron side frames. There are three steel cross rods that are staked in place in the side frames and they hold the assembly together. The barrel is bored 1" diameter 2 1/8" in from the muzzle.

The earliest versions used an electrically heated platinum wire to ignite the gasses. Extra ignitors were provided. Later versions had a steel rod staked in the breech between the tapped holes.

The rod was flush on the outside but protruded into the cannon about 1 3/4". I can only assume this is one of two electrodes used for jumping an electric spark. All gas cannons used a dry cell battery and acetylene generator similar to that described in Franklin's patent.

The operating manual for this cannon is twelve pages long. The wooden box the toy was shipped in becomes the housing for the acetylene generator and holder, the battery, the pinch cock, the rheostat, and the switch.

The top part of the acetylene generator is called the holder and it is it's weight bearing down on the gas that provides the pressure to move the gas to the gun. The dimple in the bottom of the generator is one of the features in Franklin's patent. The lump of carbide, dropped through the charging tube is deflected to the side by the dimple thus the rising gas gets trapped in the holder instead of escaping out the charging pipe.

The user is cautioned to be sure to charge and bleed the acetylene generator in order to purge any oxygen that may be in there. An explosive atmosphere in the holder and supply tube is like a bomb with a fuse.

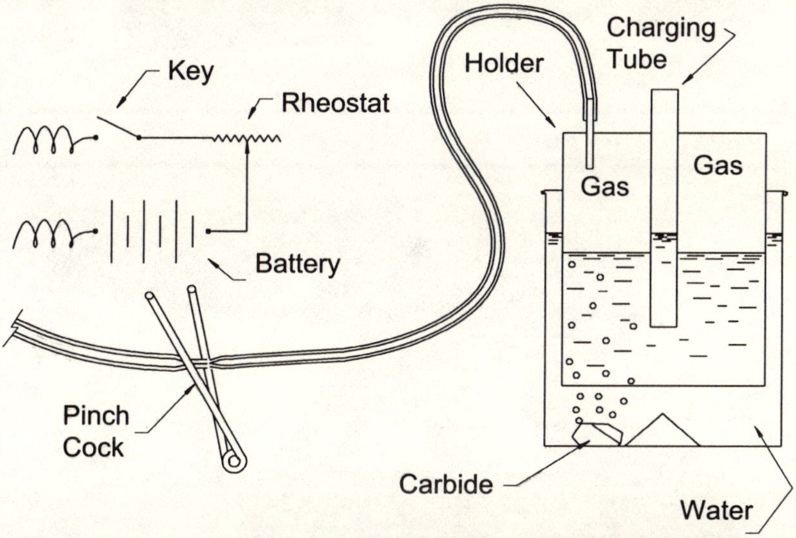

The pinch cock is used to regulate the gas supply to the cannon. The weight of the holder determines the gas pressure and therefor the time required to charge the cannon. A generator-holder made from close fitting soup cans requires two seconds with the cock open to charge the gun.

Before connecting the gas hose to the gun it is necessary to adjust the rheostat. The rheostat is used to control the current to the platinum wire. Too much and the wire burns out, not enough and no ignition. The manual reads: "Move the slider to the extreme end of the rheostat. Then press the key repeatedly, and, looking in at the muzzle of the gun, adjust the slider until the igniter becomes cherry red when the key is depressed."

The explosion creates a vacuum in the cannon and air rushes in to fill this vacuum and this is how the oxygen gets replaced between firings. After each shot the gas cock is opened for the charging period. The gas is allowed to mix with the air in the cannon for another five or ten seconds and then it is fired.

"An Ideal Fourth of July Toy, The Gas Cannon."

Price Guide Gas Cannon
Poor - $25 - $75
Good - $75 - $250
In Box - $250 - $500
New Prices: Unknown

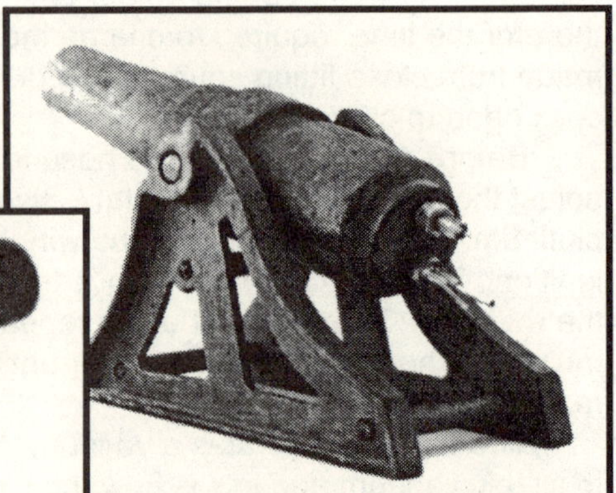

6F-FIELD ARTILLERY

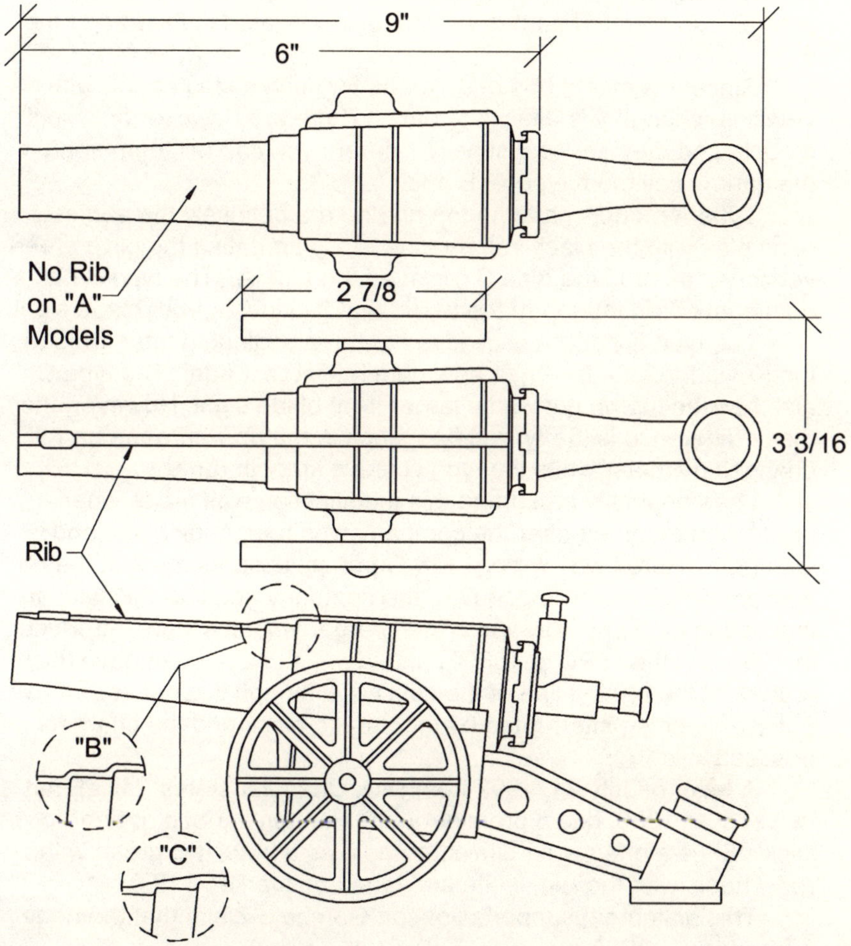

6F - Field Artillery, 1929-1941, 1947-1952, 1955-Present
Quantity: Estimated over 5 million (includes 60MM)

Markings: None
Wheels: 2 7/8" diameter, rib on both sides
Breech: Breech Plate
Breech block: Bayonet
Ammo Chest: Integral
Weight: 2 Lbs.

The 6F is a cast iron one piece cannon using the bayonet breach block with pressed steel breach. Wheels are iron and the ammunition compartment is integral being located in the end of the drag.

Since this model has been made for such a long period with very little change it is difficult to date. There are however 3 distinct models and they are so distinctly different you can tell them apart in the dark. I call them type A, B and C.

Type A models have no top rib and are definitely the earliest examples with the black variety most likely predating the olive green versions. In 1935 the type B replaced the type A. The type B has a dominant rib on the top of the barrel that includes a front blade sight.

The type C pattern is believed to have originated after 1955 at the Keystone foundry when new patterns were made. The type C also has the top rib but with a larger front blade sight. However, the major difference is the type B has steps in the rib where the barrel changes diameter while the type C has a smooth ramp.

I had originally presumed this modification was made when production resumed after the company was bought by Miller and Gombotz. Here I was wrong. Mr. Gombotz assures me that the rib was on the 6F when he acquired the company and that this was an innovation made by Wily when the charger versions were introduced in 1935. All the 10FC's, 15FC's and 15AC's I have seen have this feature at the parting line of the casting, although it is not as noticeable being interrupted by the breech block and the charger bosses.

A letter of July 24, 1992 from Dick Chandler states "My 6F not newer than 1936, has a prominent *ridge* on top surface or barrel." Dick's 6F is a one owner since he had it as a boy. It is green with red wheels with the red, white and blue box marked $1.50.

This statement supports Joseph Gombotz' claim that the ridge was added in 1935.

If you have the original box or other documents then you can get a better idea of its vintage based on the prices. If you have the red, white and blue box then it is definitely pre-war. Mr. Gombotz assures me that since he first worked for Wily in 1946 only the green boxes were used.

This type B 6F came in a green box at $4.95 which puts it about 1962.

This 6F is olive green with no top rib. The box it came in is red, white and blue. Lack of a top rib puts the cannon pre 1935 and the red, white and blue box is pre WWII.

Price Guide 6F
Poor - $20 - $30 Only for pre-1935 (no rib)
Good - $20 - $60
MIB - $40 - $100
New Costs: 1929/1941 $1.50, 1942 - $2.00, 1956 - $3.95, 1962 - $4.95, 1980 - $14.95, 1981 - $15.95, 1986 - $19.95, 1989 - $24.50, 1990 - $25.95, 1991 - $29.95, 1992/1993 $39.95.

60MM-FIELD ARTILLERY

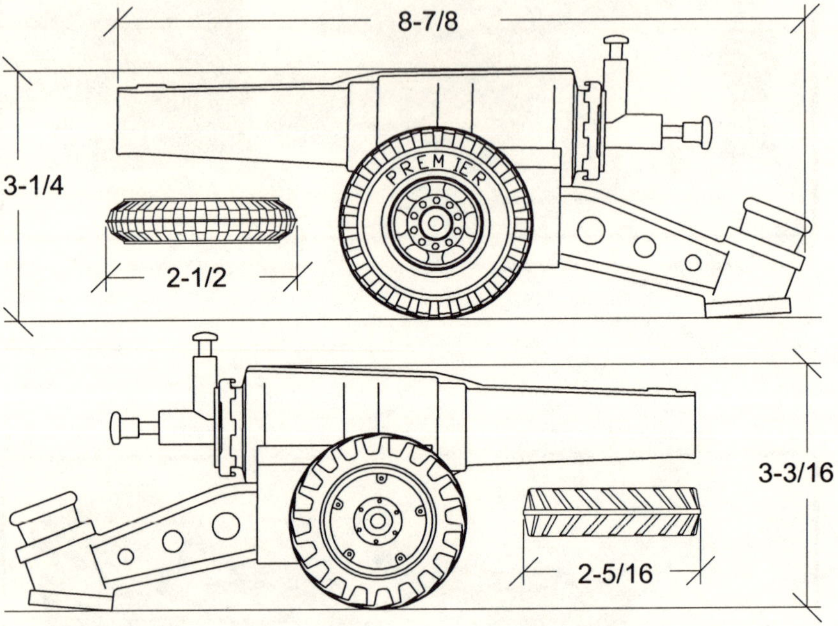

60MM - Field Artillery, 1958 - Present

The 60MM is the result of a trickle down from the Millers wanting something new. The same wheels used on the 155MM and 105MM were then applied to the 6F and it became the 60MM.

The versions with the PREMIER tires are the earliest. These wheels required a portion of the hub to be machined away and eventually the move was made to the tractor type tires which needed no re-work. Both versions are plentiful but the PREMIER tire ones are getting harder to find. A 60MM could use either the “B” or “C” type casting (see 6F).

Weight: 2 Lbs. 2 Oz.

Price Guide 60MM
Poor - Don't bother, plenty of good ones around.
Good - $20 - $30
In Box - $30 - $60
New Prices: 1958 - $3.95, 1975 - $9.95, 1980 - $14.95, 1981 - $15.95, 1986 - $19.95, 1989 - $24.50, 1990 - $25.95, 1991 - $29.95, 1993 - $39.95.

This 60MM has the Premier tires (casting is type B).

This 60MM has the tractor type tires (casting is type C).

5T- ARMY TANK

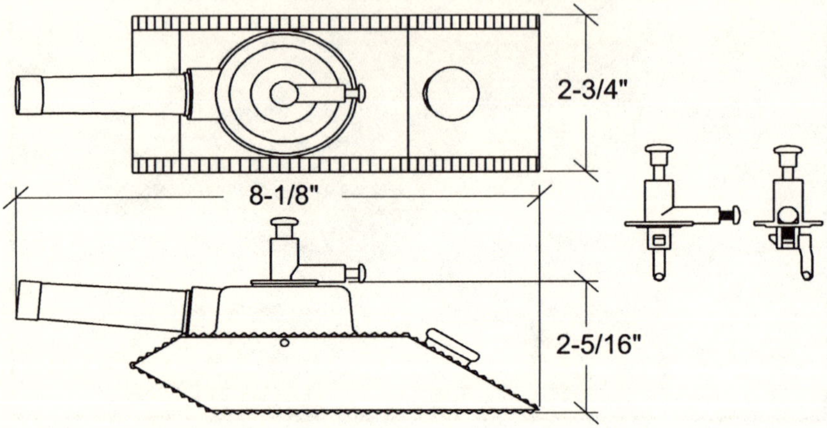

5T - Army Tank 1926 - 1935 💣💣

Markings: 5-T, on top of turret.
Breech: Bayonet
Breech block: Bayonet with small measure.

The little 5-T Army Tank was introduced as "The Baby of the Big-Bang Family" in 1926 and retailed for $1.00. The body of the tank is fir or pine with embossed tin tracks tacked on.

The tracks do a fine job of armoring the wood on the bottom and corners. A large hole is bored in the block for the turret assembly which is secured in place by two tacks. A smaller hole in the rear sloping deck forms the ammunition compartment.

The turret assembly is made up of two die-cast pieces, a top and a bottom with a rolled steel barrel pressed in. The barrel is finished at the muzzle with a brass collar. Inside the turret there is a tin baffle between the combustion chamber and the barrel. The tank is finished in a light grey.

The 5-T is the first BIG-BANG to use the bayonet type breech and breech block. The 5-T breech block is unique among the bayonet breech blocks because of it's spoon design and is worth more because the common bayonet breech block cannot be substituted.

Standard Bayonet Breech Block (Left), 5T Breech block (right).

Price Guide 5TA
Poor - $25 - $35
Good - $35 - $50
In Box - $50 - $100
New Prices: 1926 - $1.00, 1930/1931 $1.00

5T-MOTOR TANK

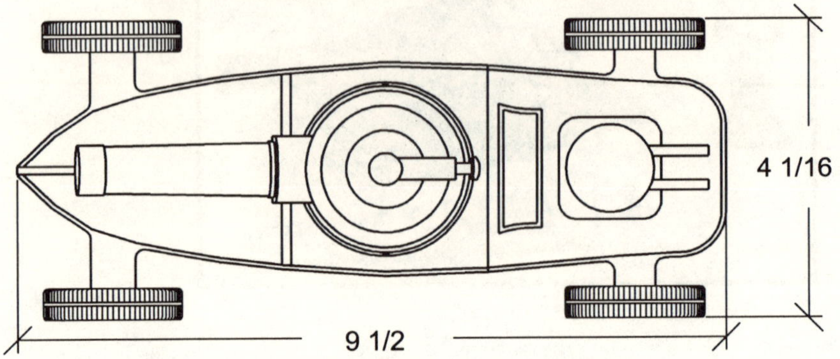

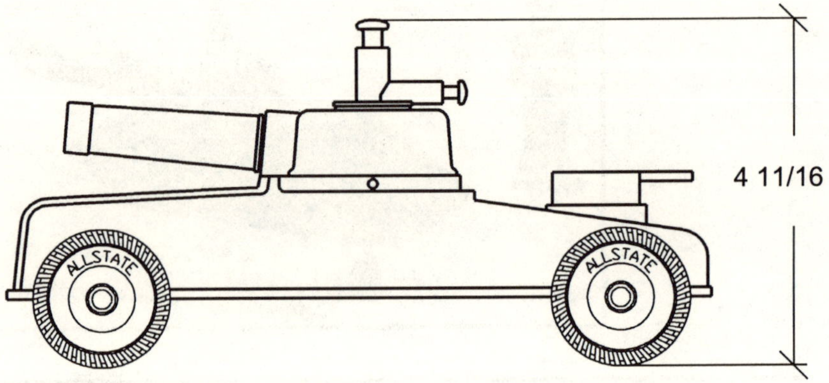

5T - Motor Tank, 1941 - 1965

The Motor Tank has the same catalog number as the earlier 5T Army Tank and shares the same turret and barrel. This is where the similarity ends. The Motor Tank has a hull of cast iron and four rubber wheels.

Markings: Turret: 5-T
Wheels: ALLSTATE
Ammo chest: Integral
Breech: Bayonet Type
Breach block: Bayonet
Weight: 3 Lbs.

Price Guide 5TM
Poor - $60 - $100
Good - $100 - $200
In Box - $200- $350
New Prices: 1945 - $2.50, 1956 - $4.45

6P-PISTOL

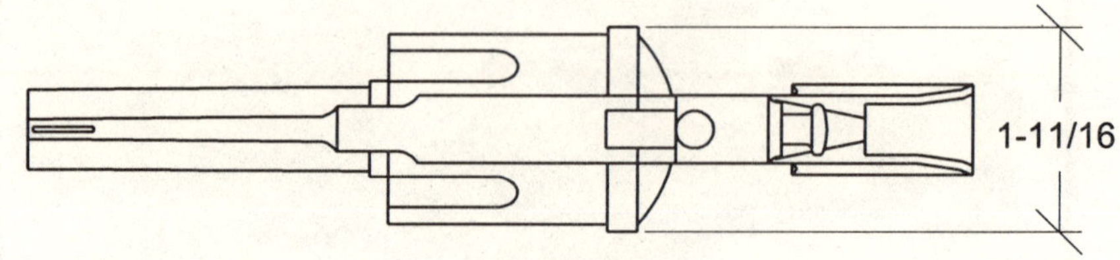

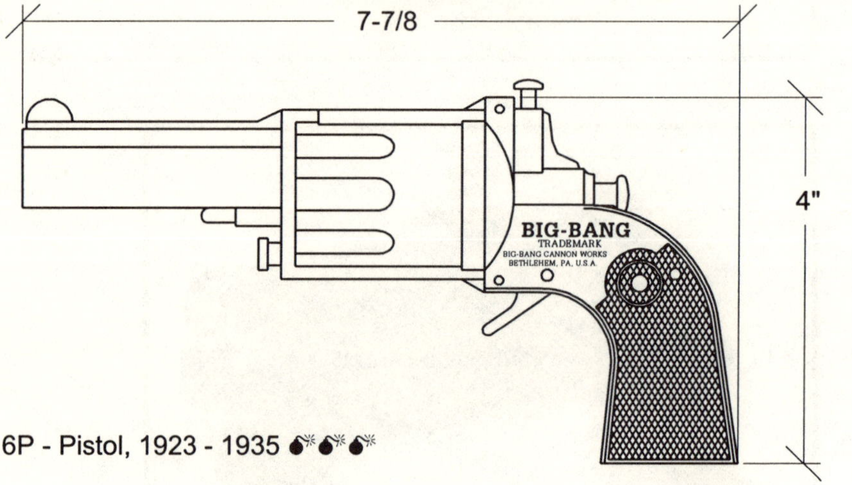

6P - Pistol, 1923 - 1935

The pistol was introduced in 1923 and was the first, but not the last, BIG-BANG to embody a form other than a cannon.

The pistol is made of five major pieces, all die-cast: The grip, the body/barrel, the trigger, the breech block and the ammunition cover. The patent indicates the two main halves could be separated for cleaning, but the toy itself is pinned tight.

The BIG-BANG pistol had a difficult time competing with cap guns. It was louder but suffered from a much lower rate of fire and had to be fired within a short time of being prepared. Nonetheless, the pistol has survived in sufficient quantities that one may hope to add one to their collection at only two or three times the cost of a cannon.

The weakest point on the pistol is the trigger. Because die-cast items get brittle with age, you should not fire the pistol by pulling the trigger. If you must fire it do so by pushing the plunger with your thumb and only fast enough to make sparks, do not “snap” it.

There is one Big-Bang brochure showing the charger models and the pistol together. This piece of evidence tells us that the pistol was still available for some time after 1935. This brochure was found with a type "A" 6F in a red, white, and blue box.

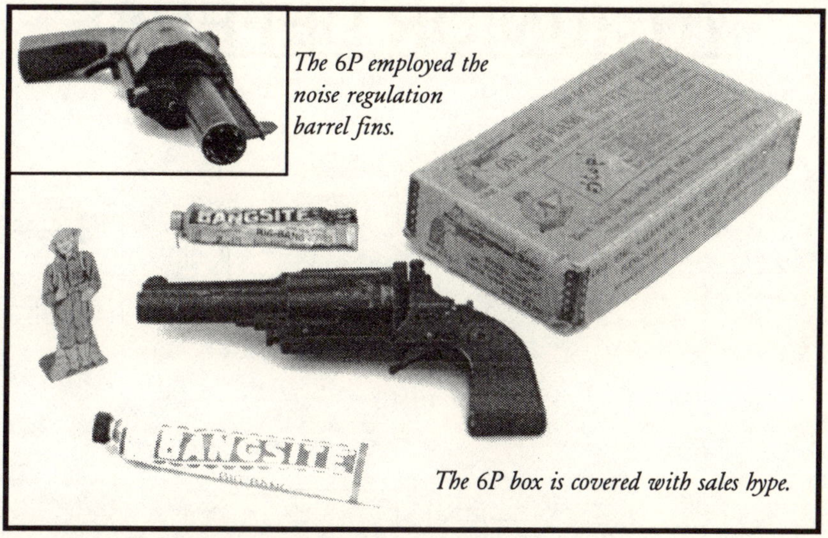

The 6P employed the noise regulation barrel fins.

The 6P box is covered with sales hype.

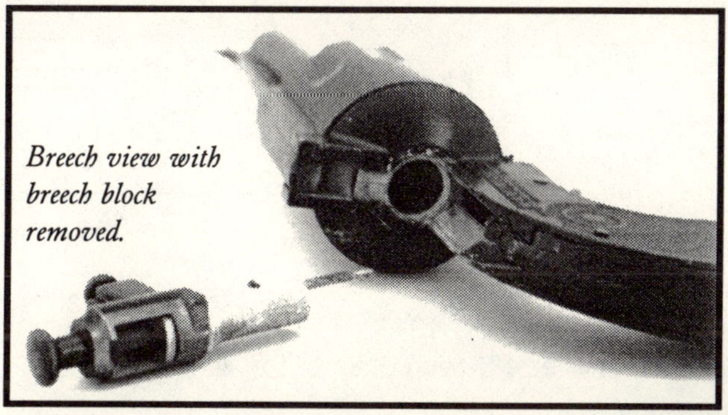

Breech view with breech block removed.

Grip hinges open to reveal magazine.

Price Guide 6P
Poor - $50 - $75
Good - $75 - $175
In Box - $175 - $250
New Prices: 1923 - $2.00, 1935 - $2.00

7D-JUNIOR DEFENSE

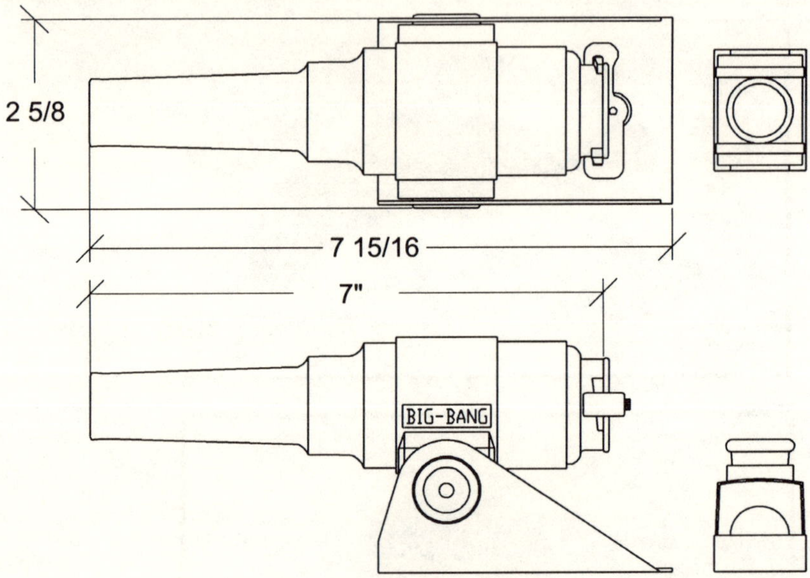

7D - Breach Loading Fixed Artillery, 1917 - 1923
With BIG-BANG in barrel 💣💣💣, with plain barrel 💣

The 7D Junior Defense is an unusual BIG-BANG in that it is the only model to have a separate ammunition chest. It uses the same barrel as the 7F but mounted in a sheet metal frame. The tilting barrel is held in position by the natural spring of the frame. The ammunition chest should have straps and the parting line should be continuous across the spot where the lugs would be on a 7F ammo chest.

Markings:
Tube Right Side: BIG-BANG
Left Side: MODEL 7
Ammo chest: 7-DAC (on bottom)
Breech: Lug Type
Breach block: Wheel Type
Weight: 2 lbs. 2 oz.

The 7D is the only model to have a separate magazine.

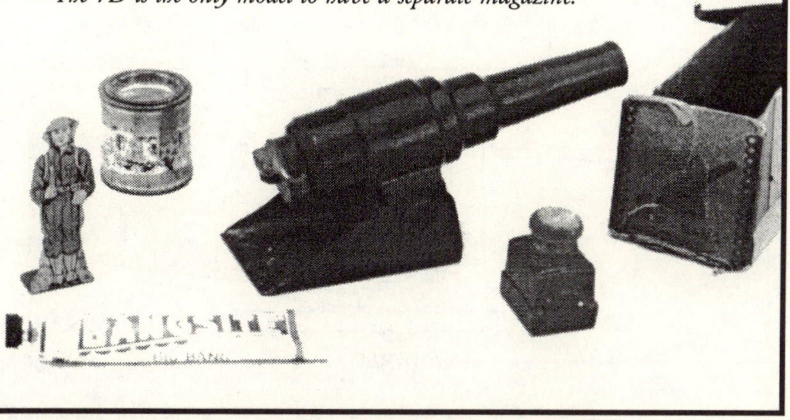

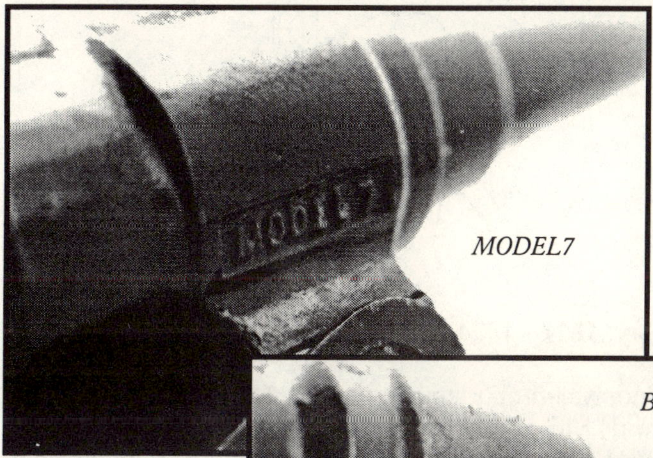

MODEL7

BIG BANG

Price Guide 7D
Poor - $25 - $35
Good - $35 - $50
In Box - $50 - $100
New Prices: 1917 - $1.00, 1918 - $1.25

7F-FIELD ARTILLERY

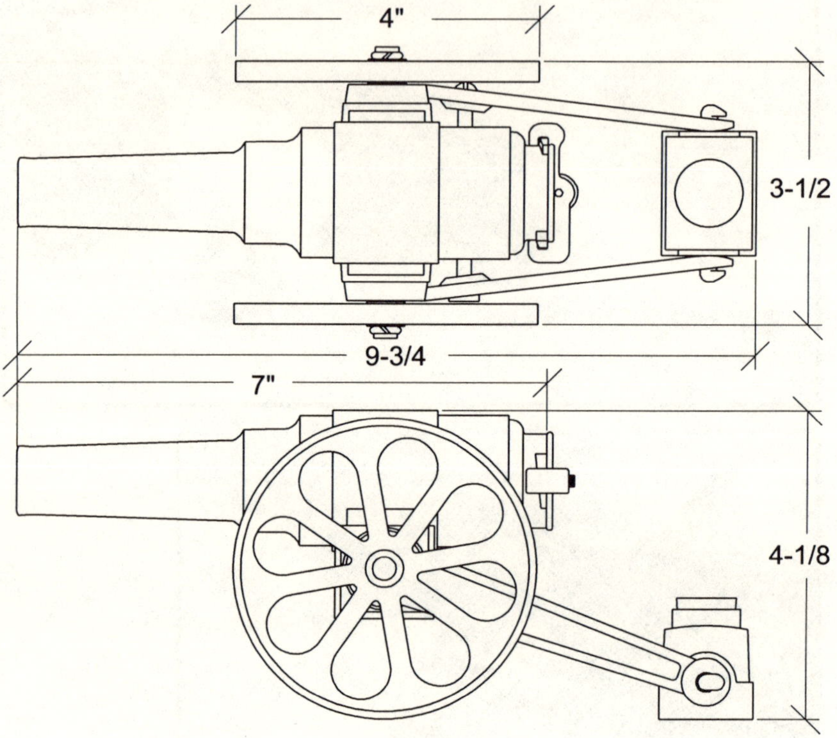

7F - Field Artillery, 1917 - 1924

This is a fine, well-proportioned cannon. The rarest examples will have the words BIG-BANG and MODEL7 in the barrel casting. As was Conestoga's custom of continuing to manufacture and ship a model after it was replaced in the line, the 7F was probably shipped into the 20's and in that case would have the plunger type ignition fitted. Some 7F's have wheels with no ribs on the spokes.

Weight: 2 lbs. 11 oz. with wheelie breech block
Wheels: 3 15/16 diameter, NO RIBS or RIBS ONE SIDE
Breech: Lug Type   Breech Block: Wheel TYPE

- MARKINGS -

Tube: Early models may have MODEL7 on one side and BIG-BANG on the other (see 7D). Later models have no markings.
Chest: 7FB

Some 7Fs have wheels with no ribs at all. These wheels have ribs on one side only.

Price Guide 7F
Poor - $50 - $75
Good - $75 - $125
In Box - $125 - $200
New Prices: 1917 - $1.50

8F-FIELD ARTILLERY

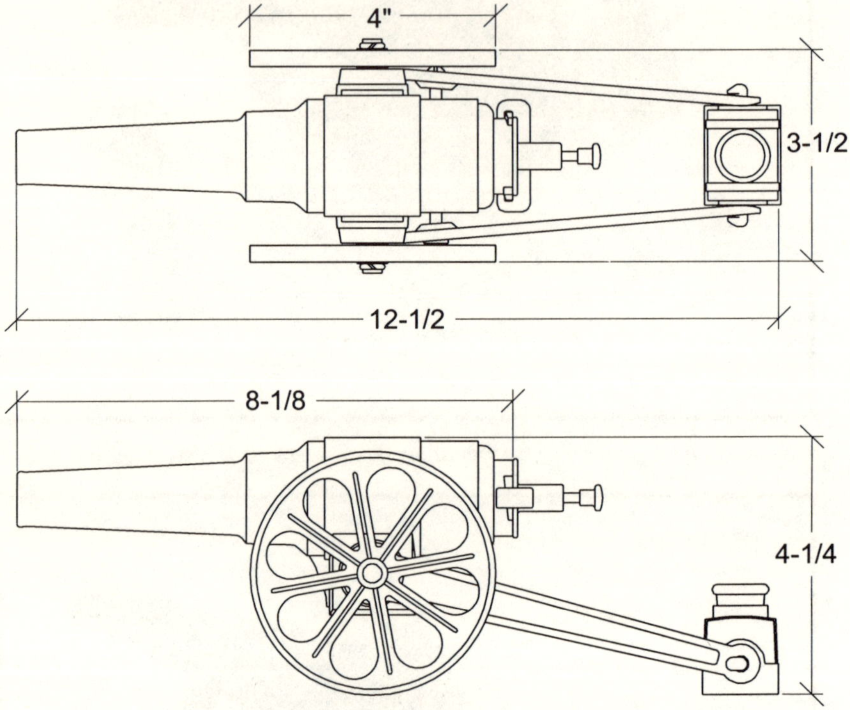

8F - Field Artillery 1924 - 1935 💣💣

The 8F - Field Artillery replaced the 7F about 1923 or 1924. The wheels and ammunition chest are the same as those on the 7F but the barrel and trails are both longer. This model was produced for eleven years until 1935.

Markings
Wheels: 8FW
Trails: 8FDB
Ammo chest: 7FAC

Breech: Lug Type Breach block: Plunger
Weight : 3 Lbs. 1 Oz.

BIG-BANG model 8F field artillery.

Price Guide 8F
Poor - $50 - $75
Good - $75 - $125
In Box - $125 - $200
New Prices: 1924 - $2.25

8FR-FIELD ARTILLERY

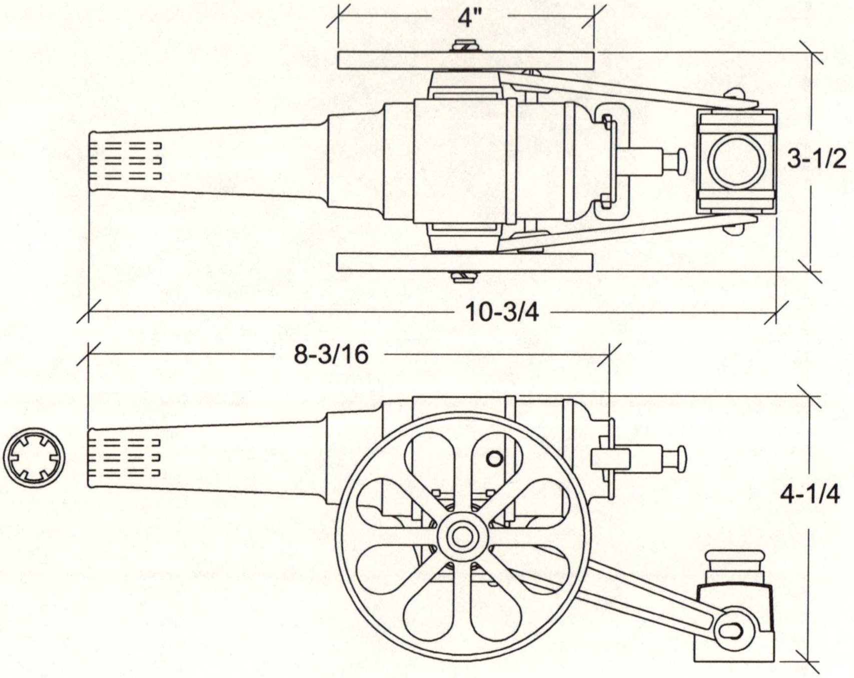

8FR - Field Artillery, 1924 - 1935 💣💣

The 8FR was introduced about the same time as the 8F. The "R" in the model designation stands for noise regulation. The cannon barrel is made up from two die-cast pieces, riveted together. The interesting thing about the design is the six internal ribs in the muzzle. I doubt that these regulated any noise; more likely they prevented the efective loading of a projectile. The wheels, drags and ammunition chest are all cast iron. The drags are from the 7F, the longer 8F drags are not needed to counter balance the lighter weight of the die-cast barrel.

Markings:
Trails: 7FDB
Ammo chest: 7FAC
Breach: Lug Type Breech Block: Plunger
Weight: 2 Lbs. 4 Oz.

BIG-BANG model 8FR, noise regulation .

The muzzle fins on the noise regulation models effectively deterred the use of projectiles.

Price Guide 8FR
Poor - $40 - $60
Good - $60 - $125
In Box - $125 - $175
New Prices: 1929 - $2.50

9B-NAVY GUN BOAT

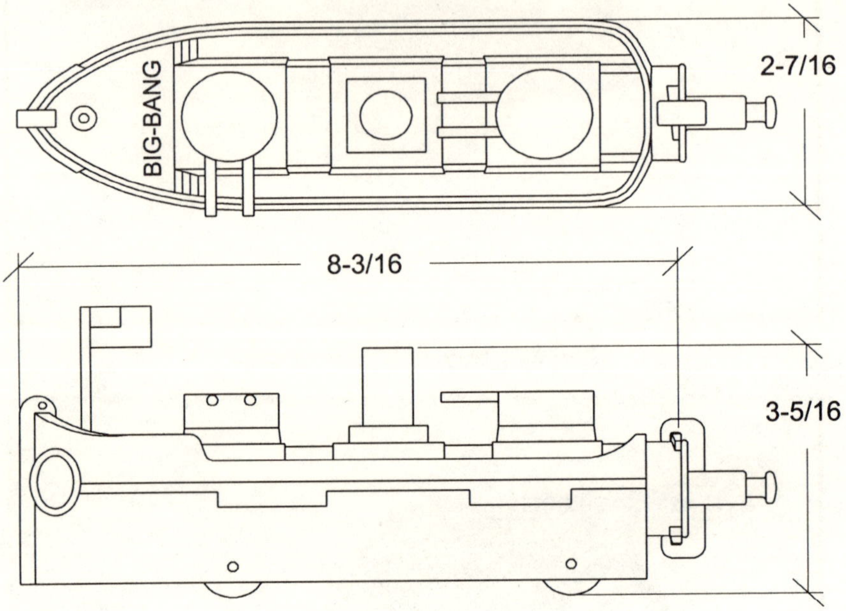

9B - Navy Gun Boat, 1924 - 1935

The Gun Boat is an interesting piece. It produces a much louder report than one would expect. The deception is due to the fact that the entire boat is the barrel. This makes it comparable with the 8F in internal volume. The hawse pipes are the muzzles and the discharge is angled out and down. When the gun boat is fired, it resembles a snorting bull.

The boat is harder to find than the Bombing Plane, but can be had for a lot less money. Loose pieces are the smoke stack, the two turrets, the flag and pole and of course, the breech block.

Markings: BIG-BANG
Breach: Lug Type Breech block: Plunger Type
Weight: 3 Lbs. 5 Oz.

BIG-BANG model 9B-Navy gun Boat.

Topsides with tin parts removed.

Bottom view, 9B -Navy Gun boat.

Price Guide 9B
Poor - $60 - $150
Good - $150 - $300
In Box - $300- $500
New Prices: 1924 - $2.00

10FC-FIELD ARTILLERY

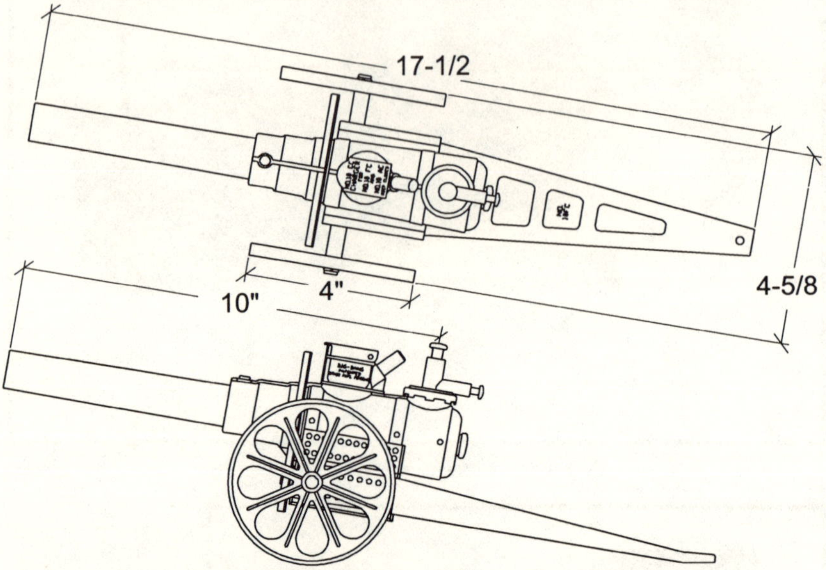

10FC - Field Artillery, 1935 - Present

The 10FC was introduced in 1935 along with the 15FC and 15AC models. The new design did away with the charging spoon and separate ammo chest. The Bangsite is now stored in a removable hopper on top of the cannon just forward of the now vertical breech block. The carbide is introduced into the cannon via a slotted plunger. When the plunger is up the slot fills with Bangsite from the hopper. When the plunger is depressed the slot carries the charge into the gun where it falls into the water sump. The new charging system makes it much easier to load the gun in the dark (important to kids). The breech block still had to be removed for ventilation between shots. Another improvement in these new models is little known. The cannon body is divided between the main area, under the charger, and the pre-ignition chamber, under the breech block, by a baffle.

The idea is that the charge is sized to produce an acetylene rich mixture. The pre-ignition area would have a less rich mixture as the gas crowds the air back. When the pre-ignition charge is fired it forces much of the gas out of the gun un-burnt. Once out of the gun it mixes with the air there and then explodes producing a louder report and more spectacular flash.

Weight: 3 Lbs. 2 Oz.

BIG-BANG model 10FC.

Price Guide 10FC
Poor - Don't bother, plenty of good ones around
Good - $20 - $40
In Box - $40 - $100
New Prices: 1945 - $3.25, 1956 - $6.95, 1958 - $8.95, 1975 - $16.75, 1980 - $23.95, 1981 - $24.95, 1986 - $37.95, 1989 - $49.95, 1990 - $51.95, 1991/1993 - $59.95.

105MM-FIELD ARTILLERY

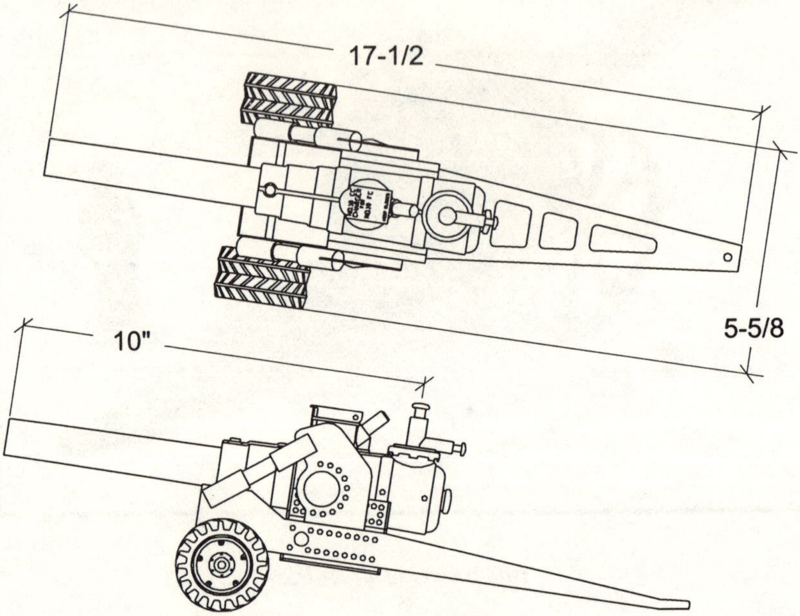

105MM - Field Artillery, 1958 - Present

The 105MM is the result of the 10FC being modernized by the addition of a new carriage. The Millers wanted something new and they got it. Designed by a Conestoga draftsman, the resulting cannon looked more like what was used during WWII and the Korean War. The new cannon did away with the shield, replaced the iron wheels with rubber tires and added shock absorbers like the big guns had.

Students of artillery history will be quick to point out that after indirect fire (firing at targets that cannot be seen from the gun) became possible by the use of recoil mechanizims, the shields on cannon were no longer needed because gun crews were not subject to small arms fire from the enemy.

So the new line looked more like the modern artillery we are used to seeing in the news reels. This new look surely added play value to the toy.

Weight: 2 Lbs. 14 Oz.

BIG-BANG model 105MM.

Label on barrel warns the user not to look into the barrel when firing the cannon.

Price Guide 105MM
Poor - Don't bother, plenty of good ones around
Good - $20 - $40
In Box - $40 - $60
New Prices: 1958 - $9.95, 1975 - $19.75, 1980 - $23.95, 1986 - $37.95, 1989 - $49.95, 1990 - $51.95, 1991/1993 - $59.95.

10W-HEAVY ARTILLERY

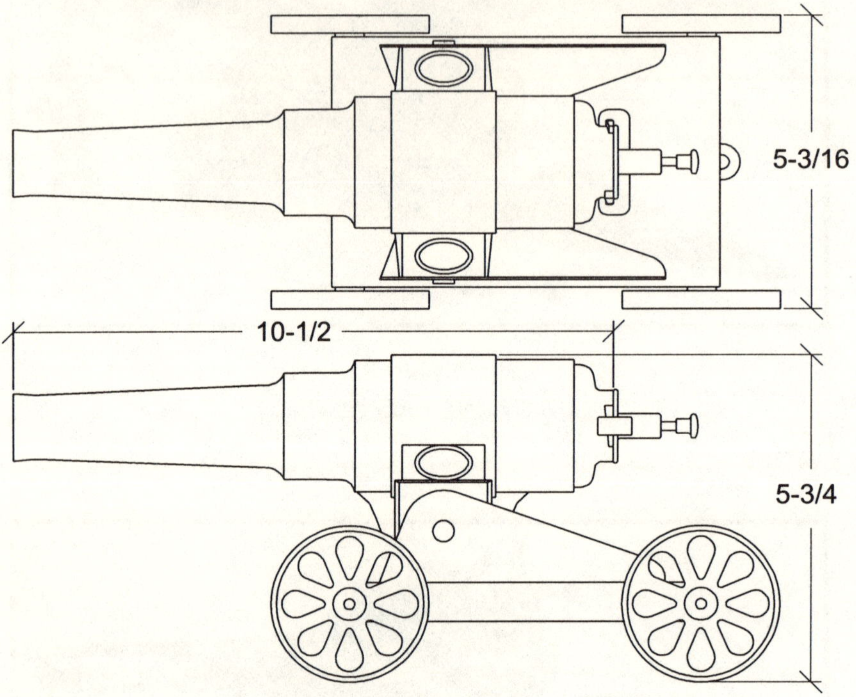

10W - Heavy Artillery, 1923 - 1935
With Tear-Drop Wheels 💣💣💣, With Pie-Slice Wheels 💣💣

In 1924 Wily took the 11D and added four wheels and a steel rod reinforcement to the sheet metal base and called it the 10W, HEAVY ARTILLERY. It is the first BIG-BANG cannon to use the new plunger type ignition developed for the pistol.

This cannon is very pleasing to the eye and is a popular toy for non-cannon collectors. It has nice proportions and the pull-toy-look makes it seem older than it is.

The original advertisement in Playthings 1924 shows the cannon with, what I call, the tear-drop wheels. For unknown reasons these wheels were not produced in great quantity and the 10W soon had the more common pie-slice wheels fitted. The version with the tear-drop wheels is hard to find and is much sought after by BIG-BANG collectors.

Markings: None
Breech: Lug Type Breach block: Plunger
Weight: 4 Lbs. 8 Oz.

The BIG-BANG model 10W was introduced with the tear-drop wheels.

10W with the tear-drop wheels (left) and pie-slice wheels (right).

Price Guide 10W (Triple for tear drop wheels)
Poor - $40 - $50
Good - $50 - $100
In Box - $100 - $150
New Prices: 1924 - $3.00, 1930/1931 - $3.00

11D-MAJOR DEFENSE

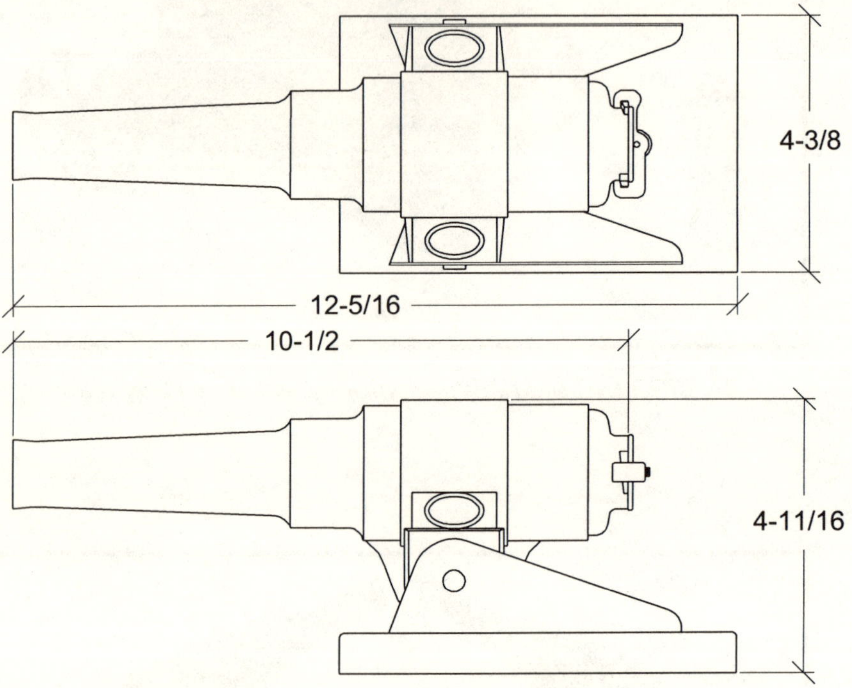

11D - Major Defense, 1917 - 1923

The 11D, MAJOR DEFENSE, is the first attempt by Wily to incorporate the magazine in the same casting as the barrel. This complicated the casting process because now two cores were required instead of one.

To accommodate the magazine sharing the space with the water sump and to leave adequate room for magazine access, the sump/magazine area of the barrel casting is considerably wider than that of the barrel on the 11F.

Markings: Early examples may have had BIG-BANG in barrel.
Breech: Lug Type Breach block: Wheel Type
Weight: 4 Lbs.

BIG-BANG model 11D, magazine side.

BIG-BANG model 11D, side opposite magazine.

Price Guide 11D
Poor - $25 - $35
Good - $35 - $50
In Box - $50 - $100
New Prices: 1917 - $2.50

11F-FIELD ARTILLERY

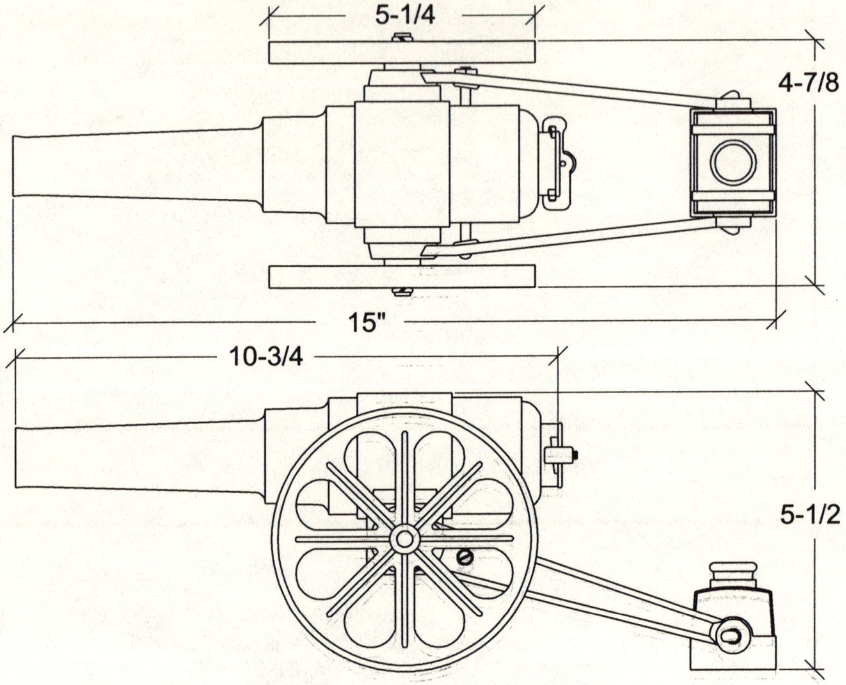

11F - Field Artillery, 1917 - 1923 💣💣

The 11F MAJOR FIELD CANNON was Wily's first all iron field piece. It is wonderfully proportioned and is the piece that the "kid" is testing his hand with. Like the 11D the 11F is advertised showing BIG-BANG in the barrel but we have never seen such an example.

Markings: Early examples may have had BIG-BANG in barrel.
Wheels: 11FW
Trails: 11FD
Ammo chest: 11FAC
Breech: Lug Type Breach block: Wheel Type
Weight: 5 Lbs.

BIG-BANG model 11F. This one is fitted with the interchangeable plunger breech block.

Price Guide 11F
Poor - $75 - $100
Good - $100 - $175
In Box - $175 - $250
New Prices: 1917 - $3.00

12F-FIELD ARTILLERY

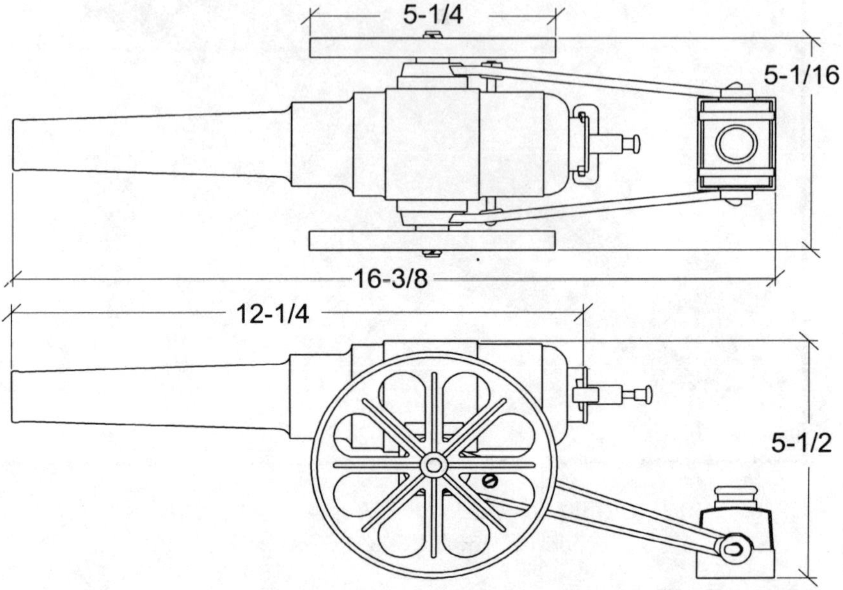

12F - Field Artillery, 1924 - 1935

The 12F is a very well proportioned cannon. It is also the most difficult to find of all the iron field pieces.

Markings:
Wheels: 12FW
Trails: 12FDB
Ammo chest: 11FB
Breech: Lug Type Breach block: Plunger.
Weight: 4 Lbs. 11 Oz.

Price Guide 12F
Poor - $75 - $100
Good - $100 - $175
In Box - $175 - $250
New Prices: 1924/1929 - $3.75, 1932 - $4.45

BIG-BANG model 12F.

12FR-FIELD ARTILLERY

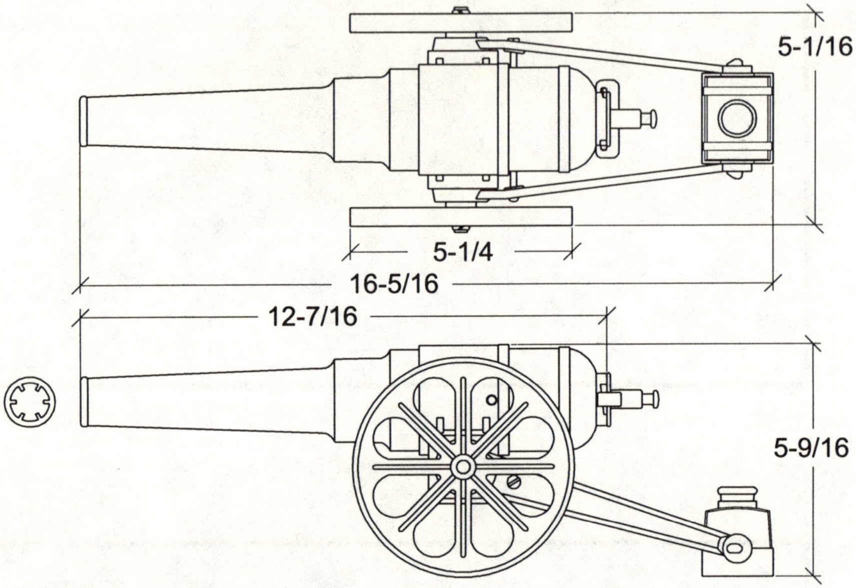

12FR - Field Artillery, 1924 - 1935

The 12FR - Field Artillery, incorporates a two piece die-cast barrel with internal fins at the muzzle. The two piece design is necessary for the die-casting process. The pieces are riveted in three places. The fit is precise and no gasket is fitted so these models experience minor leaks at the joint.

The "R" in the model number may refer to the word regulation as these models were know as the NOISE REGULATION models. The fins do little to regulate noise. What they most effectively discourage is charging the tube with a projectile.

Markings:
Wheels: 12FW
Trails: 12FDB
Ammo chest: 11FB
Breech: Lug Type Breach block: Plunger.
Weight: 4 Lbs. 11 Oz.

Price Guide 12FR
Poor - $50 - $75
Good - $75 - $150
In Box - $150 - $200
New Prices: Unknown

BIG-BANG model 12FR, Noise Regulation.

15AC ANTI-AIRCRAFT ARTILLERY

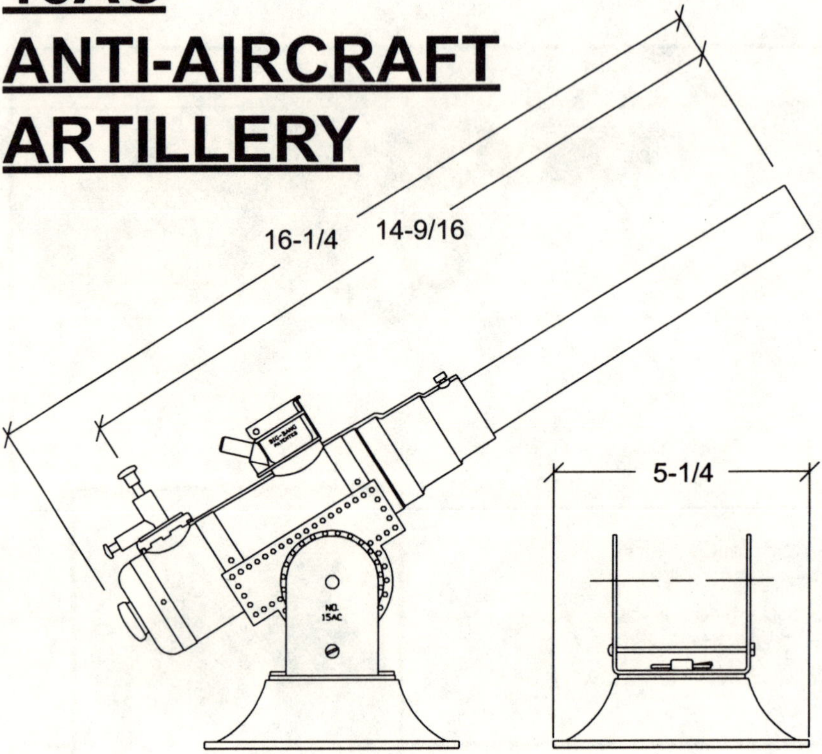

15AC - Anti-Aircraft Artillery, 1935 - 1964

The 15AC is the fifteen inch charger gun on a pedestal mount. It is the only BIG-BANG that can be both elevated and rotated. Outside of the mounting, the gun uses the same parts as the 15FC and 155MM. The mount consists of a cast iron base with a "U" shaped sheet metal frame that grips the cannon trunions and pivots on a post that is part of the base. A cotter pin secures the mount and a thin brass disk provides a bearing of sorts. A screw across the frame provides tension adjustment for the cannon elevation. The cannon casting has an area underneath where the parting line bead is absent. The frame screw passes through this void and is a stop to limit the elevation from level to about forty degrees.

According to Mr. Gombotz, this item was not a good seller. No doubt it was continued in the catalog because it required so few unique parts.

Markings: No. 15AC stamped in sheet metal frame.
Weight: 4 Lbs. 10 Oz.

Price Guide 15AC
Poor - $20- $40
Good - $40 - $75
In Box - $75 - $150
New Prices: 1945 - $4.25, 1956 - $8.45

15FC-FIELD ARTILLERY

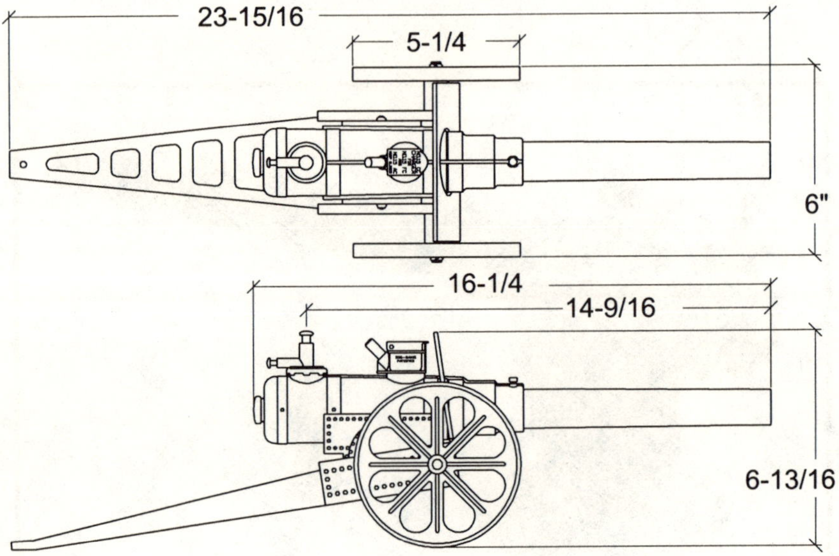

15FC - Field Artillery, 1935 - Present 💣

The 15FC is now, and was in 1935, the premier BIG-BANG. It is the largest BIG-BANG, beating the 16F by almost an inch in barrel length and by more than one and a half inches in total length. At only about half the weight of the 16F, this new model represented a substantial material savings over the older design. This model has a tilting barrel.

Markings: None
Weight: 5 Lbs. 9 Oz.

BIG-BANG model 15FC.

Price Guide 15FC
Poor - Don't bother, plenty of good ones around
Good - $30 - $50
In Box - $50 - $125
New Prices: 1935 - $4.00, 1945 - 5.50, 1962 - $12.95, 1975 - $29.75, 1980 - $31.95, 1981 - $33.95, 1986 - $48.95, 1989 - $63.95, 1990 - $66.95, 1991 - $75.95, 1992/1993 - $89.95.

155MM-FIELD ARTILLERY

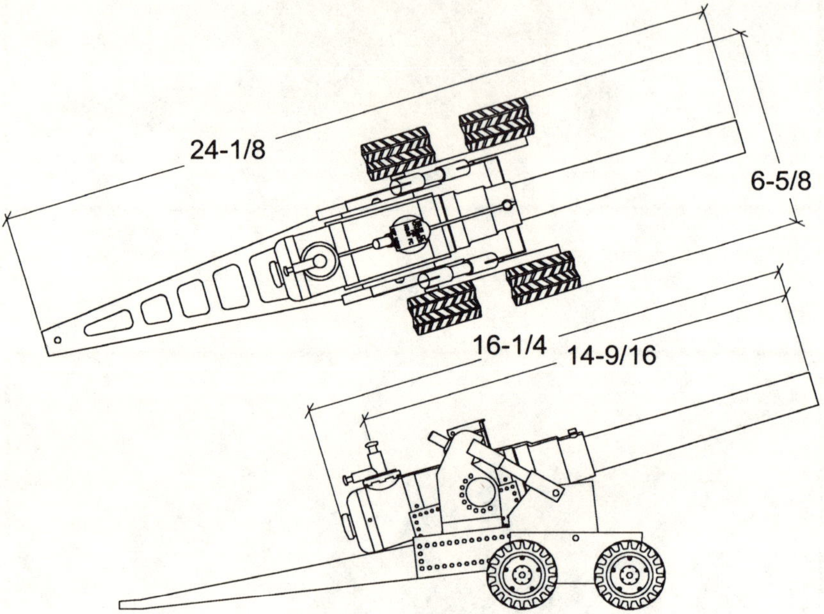

155MM - Field Artillery, 1958 - Present

Probably the first BIG-BANG to be modernized, the 155MM is patterned after the U.S. Army's 155MM and eight inch howitzers that both shared the same carriage. This cannon, as was the 105MM and 60MM can be found with both the Premier tires and the tractor tires. A variety of color schemes including all olive, all black and even camouflage have been available throughout the years.

Weight: 5 Lbs. 3 Oz.

Price Guide 155MM
Poor - Don't bother, plenty of good ones around
Good - $30 - $50
In Box - $50 - $100
New Prices: 1958 - $14.95, 1975 - $29.75, 1980 - $31.95, 1981 - $33.95, 1986 - $48.95, 1989 - $63.95, 1990 - $66.95, 1991 - $75.95, 1992/1993 - $89.95.

BIG-BANG model 155MM.

16F
SIEGE FIELD GUN

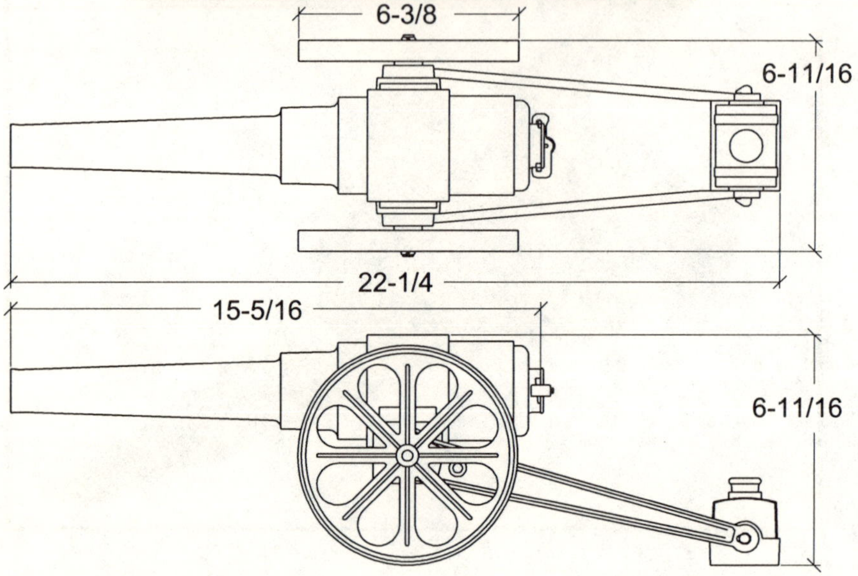

16F - Siege Field Gun 1917 - 1935

The 16F is the largest commercially produced BIG-BANG. Wily calls it the SIEGE FIELD GUN. In advertising it is stated *"This is a real Pershing Model... 16F's a beauty, the BIGGEST and LOUDEST."* My first 16F was my first old BIG-BANG. After firing a 16F there is no doubt that the *"Larger the cannon - the louder the noise."*

Probably because of it's size, more 16F's have survived than any other early model excepting perhaps the 10W. Many of these survivors will have been repaired. Of the four in my collection, all have had some type of axle replacement.

Also manufactured were the brass models, 16FYB (yellow) and the 16FRB (red). As of December 1991 the red brass version was no longer available.

Markings:
Tube: None Wheels: 16FW Trails: 16FD, 16FDB
Ammo chest: 16FA
Breech: Lug Type Breach block: Wheel or Plunger
Weight: 11 Lbs.

The BIG-BANG model 16F is an impressive cannon.

Price Guide 16F
Poor - $75 - $125
Good - $125 - $200
In Box - $200 - $300
New Prices: 1917/1929 - $3.50, 1932 - $5.50

21GG-THE G-GUN

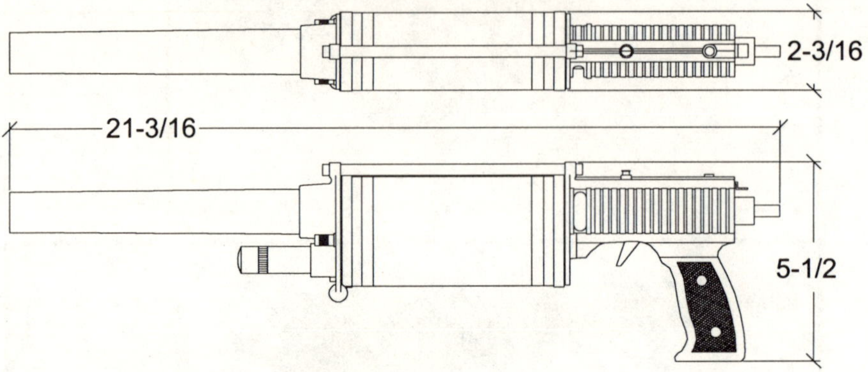

21GG - Carbide Small Arms Toy, 1936 - 1936

During the 30's Americans were looking for anything to take their minds away from the cruel reality of the depression. Along with Flash Gordon, G-Men (Government Men) were one of the big attractions. Numerous movies and more notably serials about gangsters and the men who opposed them competed for the attention of America's youth. Many toys were brought out in this period. Among these toys Conestoga's G-Gun has to rank as one of the most substantial.

Introduced in 1936, the G-Gun was the high ticket item in the BIG-BANG line, priced at $4.75, seventy-five cents more than the 15FC. Apparently the 21GG was a poor seller and it is only advertised once in Playthings. Fortunately for us, some G-Guns were made. Whether they were only a salesman's samples or part of an initial production run, the surviving G-Guns are witness to the fact that this gun went well beyond the prototype stage.

Made from cast iron, pressed steel, and brass, one look at the G-Gun should be enough to convince one that Wily was ready to equip the kids of the country with the tool to back up Eliot Ness on any occasion.

The G-Gun is very rare and very desirable.

Weight: 4 Lbs. 4 Oz.

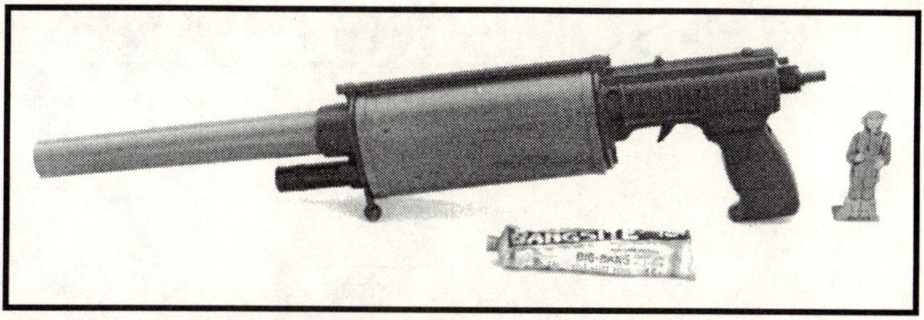

The rare and exciting BIG-BANG model 21GG, The G-Gun.

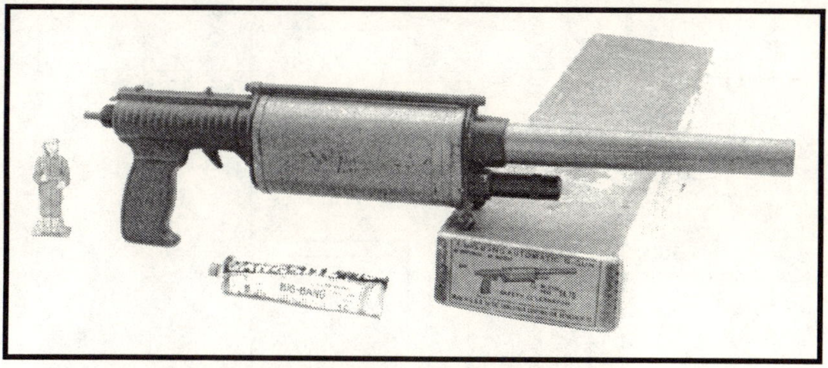

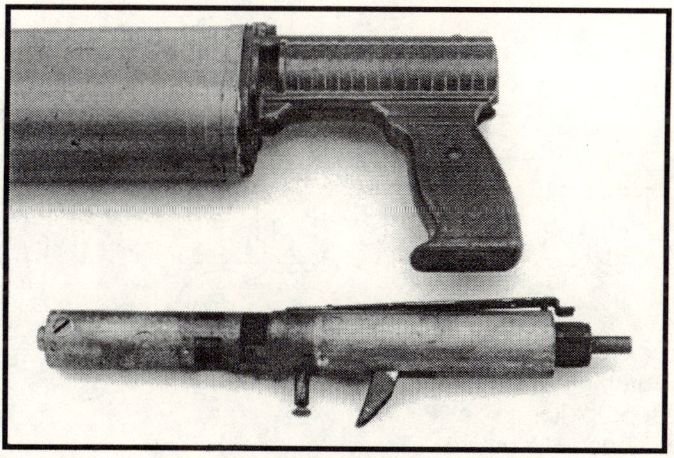

The G-Gun with bolt removed.

Price Guide 21GG
Poor - $500 - $750
Good - $750 - $1500
In Box - $1500 - $2500
New Prices: 1936 - $4.75

11P-BOMBING PLANE

Model B Bombing Plane
Weight: 5 Lbs.

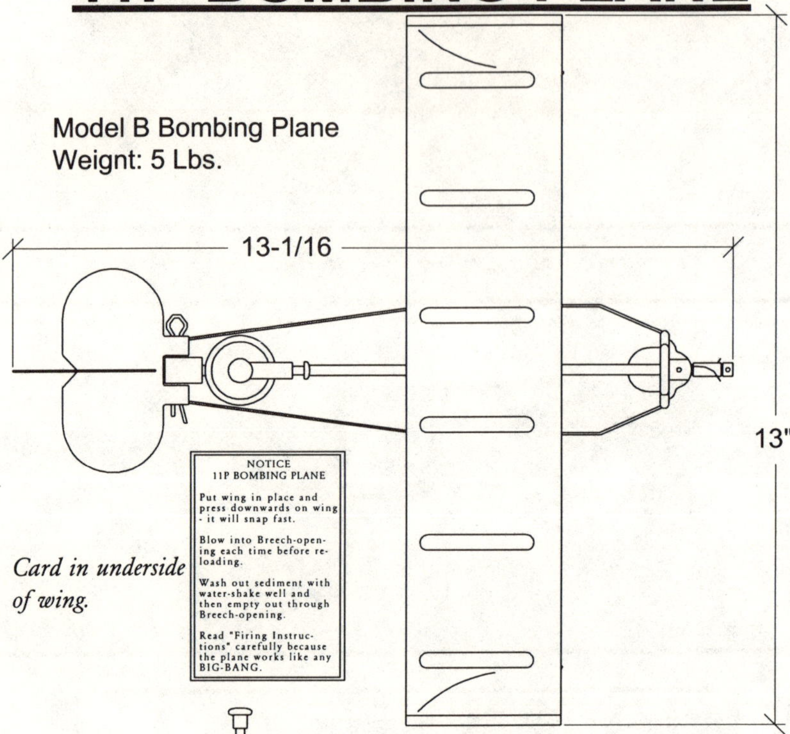

Card in underside of wing.

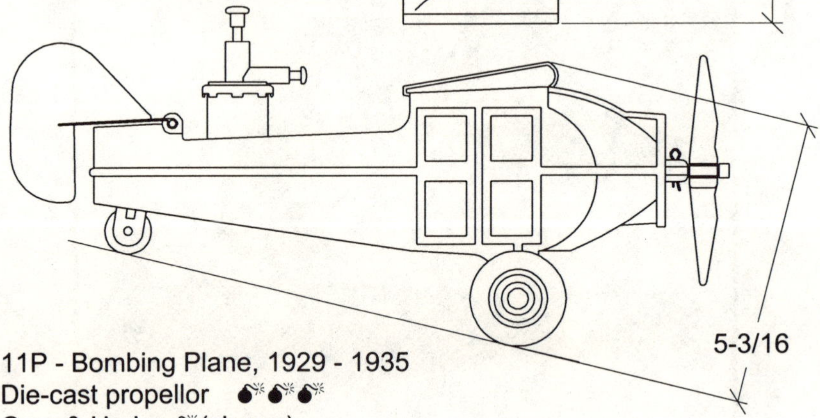

11P - Bombing Plane, 1929 - 1935
Die-cast propellor 💣💣💣
Over & Under 💣(shown)

I remember when I saw my first plane. It was at an auction preview at Southeby's in New York. The plane was part of the Kovelski collection and was mint and in the box. Green and cream and it looked like it never had water in it.

After all these years how can something survive without being played with? I marveled that the box should survive in such good shape. If a mintie has survived then there is hope for me to find an old dirty one that maybe needs a part.

Eventually I found such a plane, not dirty but the entire tail was missing. Well the tail is one of those parts that is easy to replicate so we went for it.

The early plane, I call it the model A, had a sheet metal tubular barrel that was either cast in place or pressed in after the fuselage was bored out to receive it. This tube extended from the nose to the combustion chamber.

At the nose a die-cast piece was pressed in which resembled a 4 spoke wheel with an axle protruding at the center. The gaps between the spokes were 4 vents that were the exhaust ports for the explosion. (See page 49)

Attached to the axle was a die-cast propeller that had two blades and it's center was a multibladed turbine affair that harnessed the explosion to set the propeller spinning. So two decades before the turbo-prop engine was developed Conestoga already had a gas turbine prototype! The one I saw had a grey fuselage and the pressed steel parts were black as were the wheels.

The second variation of the Bombing Plane appeared around 1931. The die-cast propeller was short lived because it was easily broken and the second variation of the plane (model B) eliminated the sheet metal barrel.

The fuselage was all iron and the casting modified for two exhaust ports in an over and under configuration. Between the two was the propeller shaft. The shape of the nose betrays the original design and one can still see where the round 1" barrel was bored in.

The shaft itself is brass and secured in a machined bore by a cotter pin. The propeller is 22 ga. steel stamped from two parts and spot welded together.

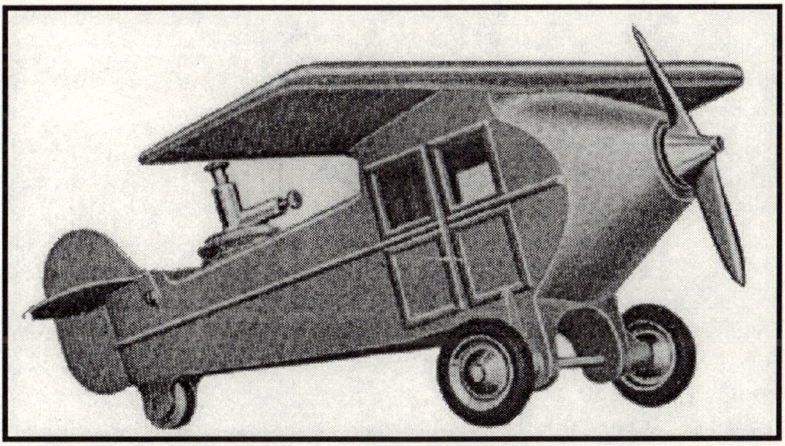

The hard-to-find model A Bombing Plane with die-cast propeller assembly.

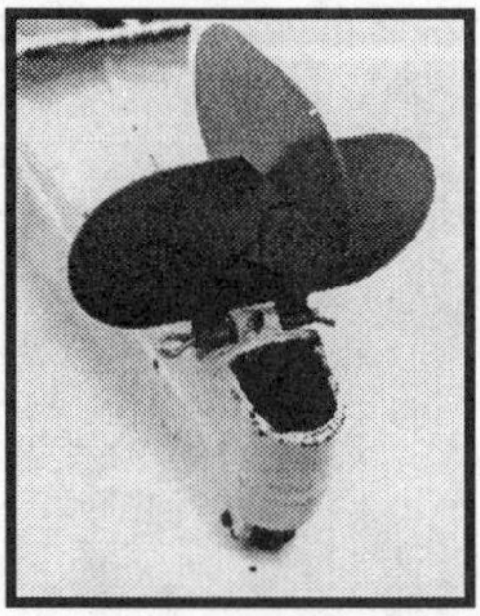

The magazine is under the hinged tail.

Price Guide 11P (add $100 for early model)
Poor - $250 - $350
Good - $350 -500
In Box - $500 - $900
New Prices: 1929 - $3.50, 1931/1932 - $2.50

Parts still available from Conestoga

Conestoga Company still offers replacement parts for all the cannons now being made as well as reproduction breech blocks for the older guns.

Powder spoons for the older guns should be ordered by length.

16F, 16FRB and 16FYB use the 4" spoon.

10W, 11F, 11D, 12F and 12FR use the 3" spoon.

7F, 7D, 8F, 8FR and Gun Boat use the 2" spoon.

Wheels for the older models are still available with the exception of the 16F and the 10W tear-drop.

6F and 10W use the 6F wheel, (2 7/8" dia.).

7F, 8F and 8FR use the 10FC wheel (4" dia.).

11F, 12F and 12FR use the 15FC wheel (5 1/4" dia.).

REPLACEMENT AXLE

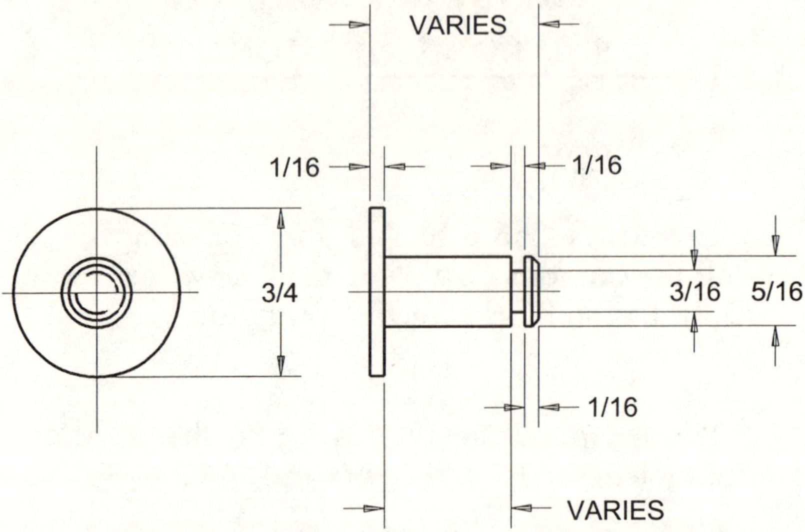

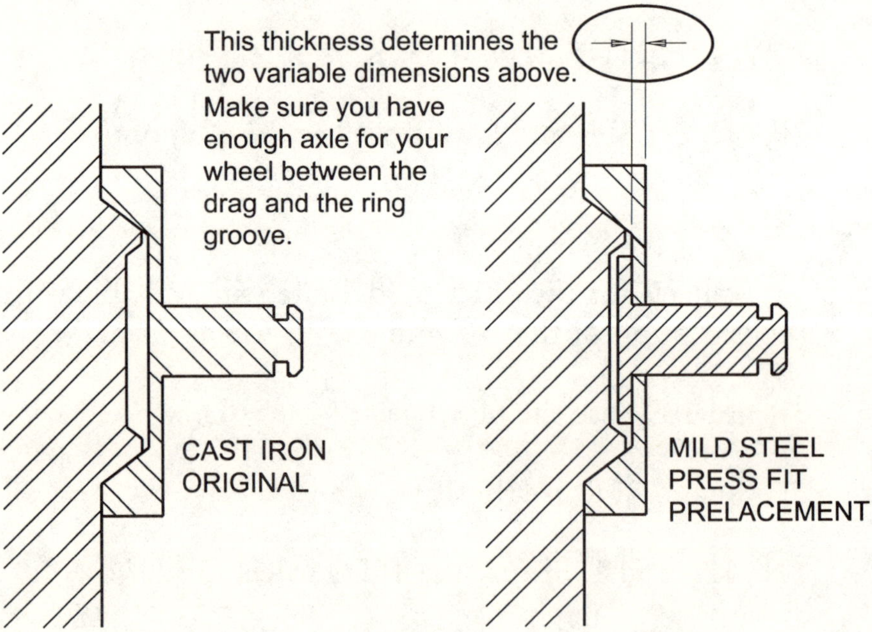

This axle repair, when done properly, is only detectable by disassembling the cannon.

EXTRA

Here are a few things that could not be woven into the fabric of the story, but could not be left out either.

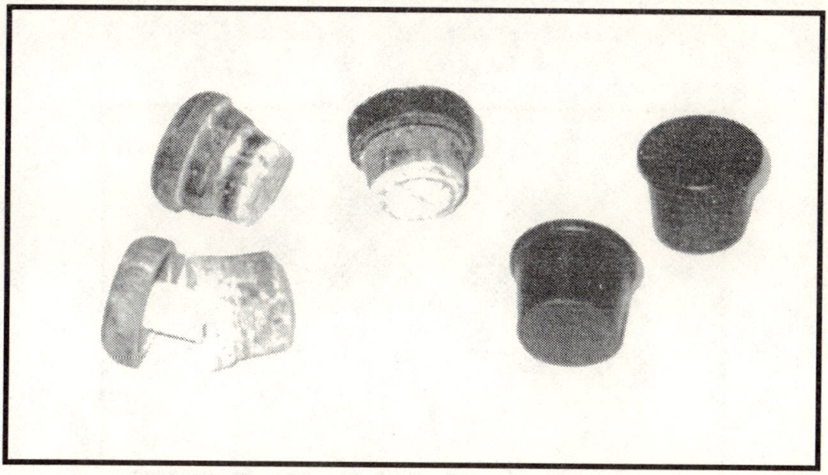

Plugs for ammo chests varied over the years. The oldest ones (two on left) were two-piece affairs. The mushroom-shaped top piece was hardwood and the stopper on the bottom was cork. The one in the center is all cork and the two on the right are the current hardwood variety.

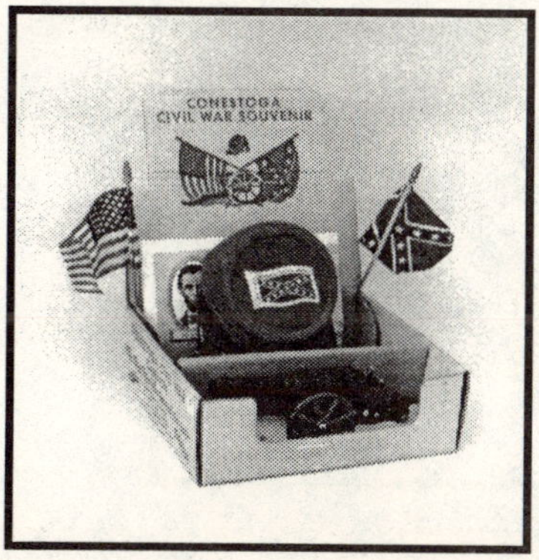

The 6F was put up in this Civil War set in the early 1960's. It was not a big seller, but a few can still be found.

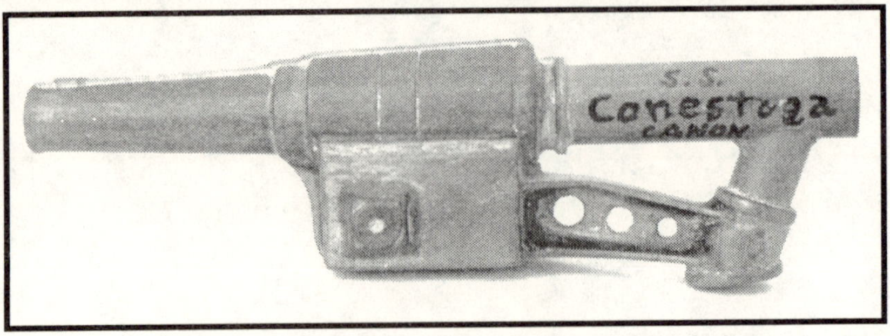

Hardwood casting pattern used to produce type "B" 6F's.

BIG-BANG model 8FR (left) and 12FR (right).

The fins in the noise regulation models above and the pins in the barrels below were both intended to prevent the cannons from throwing a projectile.

BIG-BANG model 12F (left) and 6F (right).

This is not a high school shop project. Conestoga made these lamps and they have a special non-operating breech block.

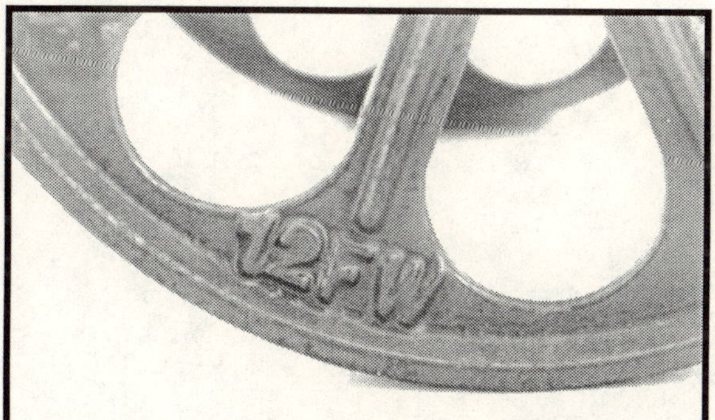

Many BIG-BANG castings are well marked as is this wheel on a model 12F.

You can't tell the players without a

SCORE CARD

Photocopy this page and keep it in your wallet for quick reference at antique markets. Collect all 27! Use this handy list to check 'em as you get 'em.

Bibliography

LETTRES DE MR. ALEXANDERE VOLTA

ALESSANDRO VOLTA AND THE ELECTRIC BATTERY
Bern Dibner, FRANKLIN WATTS, INC. NEW YORK

BETHLEHEM OF PENNSYLVANIA THE FIRST 100 YEARS
Bethlehem Book Committee, Chamber of Commerce, Bethlehem, PA, 1968

THE CHEMISTRY OF ACETYLENE
Julius A Nieuwland, C.S.C.,Reinhold Publishing Corp. New York

FOCUS, Summer/Autumn 1982 ISSUE NO. 2
Communications Department, Linde Division, Union Carbide Corp.

EPITOME
LEHIGH UNIVERSITY, BETHLEHEM, PA.

MECHANIX ILLUSTRATED
TIMES MIRROR MAGAZINES, INC., 2 Park Ave., New York, NY

PLAYTHINGS MAGAZINE
51 Madison Ave. New York, NY 10010

BOYS LIFE MAGAZINE
BOY SCOUTS OF AMERICA, 1425 Walnut Hill Lane, Irving, TX 75062

For listings of auctions, shows and sales:
ANTIQUE TOY WORLD
P.O. BOX 34509
CHICAGO, IL 60634

THE INSIDE COLLECTOR
225 MAIN STREET
NORTHPORT, NY 11768

RENNINGER'S ANTIQUE GUIDE
PO BOX 495
LAFAYETTE HILL, PA 19444

Index

Symbols

A

B

Z

ORDER FORM

Please send the following books. I understand that I may return any books for a full refund-for any reason, no questions asked.

Send **BIG-BANG CANNONS** ___ Hard cover ___ Soft cover to:

Name____

Street____

City_________________________________State________Zip_______

Send **BIG-BANG CANNONS** ___ Hard cover ___ Soft cover to:

Name____

Street____

City_________________________________State________Zip_______

Hard cover copies _________ x $27.50 = ________ . ____

Soft cover copies __________ x $19.95 = ________ . ____

Shipping and handling (see below) ________ . ____

TOTAL ENCLOSED ________ . ____

Shipping and Handling:
Book Rate: $1.50 for the first book and $1.00 for each additional book (please allow 4 to 8 weeks).
Two Day Priority Mail: $3.50 for the first book and $1.00 for each additional book.

Mail to: Ray-Vin Publishing Co.
PO Box 11435-E
New Brunswick, NJ 08906